Gail + Bo —
I'm glad you
this book! Great
for sure!

MW00352085

THEY CALL(ed) NEW CANAAN HOME

ARTHUR HAHN

God's Acre and The Congregational Church

God's Acre and The Congregational Church

The old Hahn homestead at 423 South Avenue.

(Gone, but not forgotten.)

The Edwin Eberman drawings on the front & back of this book were used with the permission of Margot (Eberman) de Ferranti.

The back cover of this book features the cupola atop what is now the New Canaan Police Department. This was formerly Saxe Junior High School.

FOREWARD

by Margot (Eberman) de Ferranti

All of us lucky enough to have been members of the NCHS class of '63 have been especially lucky to have Art Hahn in our class. We got to know Art and to know him as witty, personable and charming. He was our friend and he was everyone's friend. For those of us who attended elementary school with Art, one of the ways we knew him was as commander of all lore relating to US presidents. (Remember him in front of the class telling us that Ohio produced the most presidents – among them the heaviest at 264 pounds, William Howard Taft?) We have Art to thank for his unrelenting work in herding our class of independent individuals together for our 50th class reunion in October 2013. Since then, we have had Art to thank for following up on us regularly with emails urging us to keep our classmates in our thoughts – or, as he puts it, in our prayers.

And now we have Art to thank for this wonderful book, They Call(ed) New Canaan Home. Art has tracked down and written up the life-stories of people who lived in post-World War II New Canaan. The men and women whose life stories this book tells about deserve recognition and celebration. Their stories – some familiar, some not so familiar – are intriguing. Many are inspiring. These individuals had so much energy. So much talent. So many achievements in so many areas of endeavor. To each of the different vocations by which Art has organized this book, each person made a lasting contribution. Among the most moving are the life stories of the people we knew who are gone – NCHS classmates and teachers. Their stories are rich in personal recollections that Art went about eliciting and recording.

All together, the stories tell a story of a town and time worth remembering. It is not surprising that New Canaan, this town on the end of a railroad line leading to New York City, attracted people active in theater, journalism, radio, television, art, and business. Nor is it beyond prediction that in a book whose focus is a community the greatest number of life stories would be about community leaders and educators – members of the generation we looked to in our childhood and members of our own generation. What is surprising and unpredictable – and altogether wonderful – is that Art pursued so many people for information and memories and brought them together for us and those who come after us.

One thing more. This book offers something rewarding beyond the individual life stories and their cumulative impact. In every entry you hear Art's unique, engaging voice. He accompanies us as we read. He presents us with asides that entertain and reawaken us, providing just the right note of humor, information and humanity. Whether he is recounting the origin of an expression, injecting an opinion, inserting a personal memory, or recounting a joke, Art is with us, keeping us moving with the stories' flow, enhancing our reading experience.

So, let us give our abiding praise and thanks to Art Hahn. Although he was in our 1963 NCHS class, Art remains in a class by himself. We who know him – and all those who meet him in this book – will ever remain gladly in his debt.

PREFACE

Just what is this book about, you may be asking.

This is literally a potpourri of folks who either call, or at one time called, New Canaan home. It runs the gamut from Herb Oscar Anderson to Sloan Wilson.

Now those two names are telling. Both had prominence in their respective fields back in the 1950's & '60's. That's where much of the focus of this book will be.

Yes, there will be a scattering of some celebrities who call my hometown home today, but you're going to meet a lot of them from the past as well. For those of you who weren't born until after, say 1970, it'll be a look back at the community as it was.

You'll meet many of the COMMUNITY LEADERS of those days who made the town tick, as well as various EDUCATORS locally who encouraged our critical thinking. You'll also get to know a number of folks that went to New Canaan High School (henceforth NCHS in this tome) that went on to bigger & better things. Most of these folks were there between 1960 & 1966. Frankly I was surprised to learn about what many of them did in their adult lives.

Yes, there are a "baker's dozen" categories I profiled, from ACTORS & ACTRESSES to WRITERS & AUTHORS. You'll get to meet them individually in a casual getting-to-know-them manner, which I hope you find comfy & relaxing.

Earlier this year I got on the "If You're from New Canaan" site on Facebook when I was close to wrapping things up with this book. Even there I found help that was needed, including from a guy by the name of Bill Rogers who clued me in on the many photos of the New Canaan of yore.

True, some of you on that site were miffed that I didn't include certain people or places in there. By legal agreement, I cannot profile those that the late Warren Allen Smith had done in his 2012 tome, "Unforgettable New Canaanites", unless I have their permission. Many of you cried foul that I wasn't going to profile Joe's Pizza, but hey, that came along in 1967. I was gone from New Canaan by the autumn of 1963. So it'll be up to younger people to write their own such book down the road.

I can empathize with those people over that. Back in the fall of 2017, Karen Santry & I got chatting one night about how "WASM" (a.k.a. Warren Allen Smith) had neglected to mention a lot of people in his book. We both thought we could do a sequel, but Smith's estate was firm in saying my book had to be my own creation.

And so it is.

My late wife Nan & I were in town for my 50th NCHS class reunion in October, 2013. We'd heard good things about Joe's Pizza. "Nanson" (my pet nickname for her) craved pizza that early Saturday afternoon. Alas, Joe's was closed for some reason. I will make it a point to try it the next time I'm in town, though. Back in the day we had to journey out of town for pizza, although Phil Baker's in Norwalk had an outstanding one!

And what about Sturdivant Burpington? You failed to mention him!

Who?

Sturdivant Burpington was a character I made up while at NCHS. I thought the name sounded oh-so-elitist, so I began to get creative here. He was an independently wealthy guy who was said to take a late morning train into Grand Central on a daily basis, whiling away his time boozing it up at either the Biltmore Men's Bar, or the Commodore, or the Oyster Bar. He then went on the bar car of the 5:09 (or the 5:34, or the 6:05, or the 7:02) back to New Canaan where the conductors then poured him off the train. Rumors said that weekends he spent in the swimming pool at his house, which was filled with gin & vermouth (with a couple of jars of green olives emptied into the pool for good measure). Everyone referred to him as "Sturdy", although he never was.

However, these are real people you're meeting in these pages. Come along & enjoy getting to know them.

Oh, yes: Before we get to the acknowledgements (which most people skip over anyway), let's play Trivia! For those of you under the age of 65, please define the below listed slang terms of yore:

"Bubble Gum Machine"   "Church Key"
"Fake Out"   "Hack Session"
"Ridge Runner"   "Submarine Races"

ACKNOWLEDGEMENTS

There are many people to thank for making this book possible.

Karen Santry certainly tops the list, as she & I discussed a possible sequel to the late Warren Allen Smith's book, "Unforgettable New Canaanites". Karen did the footwork regarding permission from Smith's estate from his attorney. She & I had discussed doing such a project since the fall of 2017, but my wife's final illness put any research on this on hold until May, 2018. Karen has a very hectic schedule still going on, but her overall support for this has been most welcome by me.

Bill Gardner is a copyright lawyer still residing in New Canaan. He has been invaluable to me in that regard, providing many suggestions of names of people profiled in these pages. (Hopefully, Bill, I've dotted all my "i's" & crossed all my "t's"!)

Preston Jones was another one who provided many names as well. Both he & Karen are profiled in these pages. Both Bill & Preston have a love of New Canaan history.

Also providing names for me were various members of my class (NCHS '63), as well as members of the classes of 1960 through 1966. Lissa (Couch) Barker, Bailey Stewart, Tom Wilhelm, Patti (Liberatore) Avallone, Nancy Harding, Doug Howe, & Sandy Harlow were all instrumental in letting their classmates know about this project.

Not to mention Lisa Abrams of the Human Resources Department of the New Canaan Public Schools; Mike Murphy, the librarian of the New Canaan Historical Society; & Ms Anne Cotoia of the St. Aloysius Parish for the information they provided on various teachers, community leaders, & Sister Rita, respectively.

Thank you as well to all of you who provided both family & personal photographs for use in this publication, as well as your information about not only yourselves, but in some instances your parents & grandparents.

John & Donna Percy of Tonawanda, NY, deserve thanks for their proofreading of my manuscript. Ditto Pam Swallow (profiled herein) for doing same.

Special thanks as well to numerous folks on the Facebook site, "If You're from New Canaan...", several of whom are quoted in a few places in this book.

Then there are numerous friends who offered their love & support in encouraging me to go on with this book. So hats off to Stacia Aldret, Debi Byrd, Ronda Carter, Venusia Ellis, Chris Furr, Carl Howard, Jim Jurewicz, Margie Kimball, Brooke Rogers, Cokey Scott, & Danny Seay, all of whom reside in the Charleston (SC) area, where I currently make my home.

Kudos as well to some of my friends from my days in Buffalo, NY, who did likewise. They are Jim Baldwin, Dave Ellis, Amy Kiss, Sandie Drake Quick, Rita Rich, Amy Rockwell, & Susan Wald.

I hope I haven't left anyone out, but if I have, I do sincerely apologize.

DEDICATION

In Loving Memory of my Late Wife

NAN HENSON HAHN

1946 - 2018

AN EXTRA PROFILE

(Nan Hahn)

Yes, I called her by the pet nickname of "Nanson". Her maiden name was Henson, so it was simply a matter of using the last three letters of that name as a contraction & incorporating into her first name.

Nan was readily accepted as an honorary member of NCHS '63, even though she was a 1964 graduate of Hanover High School in Florham Park, NJ. She was fond of saying that she "was born in a Catholic Hospital & delivered by a Jewish doctor in Harlem". Her parents were primarily singers, although they did some acting professionally as well in Broadway musicals. Her father, for instance, was in the original cast of "The Most Happy Fella" in 1956. He was part of a trio that sang the song, "Standing on the Corner (Watching All the Girls Go By)", in that Frank Loesser show.

Sadly, she passed away from congestive heart failure, as well as a-fib & the failure of her kidneys, on February 12, 2018. I scattered her ashes close to her mother's grave near Portsmouth, NH, three months later. I took a much needed vacation away from Charleston, reuniting with friends & family throughout New England, NJ, northeast PA, & Buffalo then. It was while I was on the road that I decided to go ahead with writing this book. I'm most grateful that I did so.

Nan & I met when we we were students at the American Academy of Dramatic Arts during the mid-1960's. But let's hear how my late wife enjoyed telling our story:

"Arthur & I were just casual friends at the Academy. He was going with another girl & I was going with another guy. Our friendship was so casual it was like 'hi'/'goodbye' in the hallways there.

"After the Academy we both went to war. Arthur went to Vietnam & I got married.

"We lost touch with one another until the first (&, I believe, only) Academy Alumni Directory came out in the late 1980's. They had mistakenly listed me in his class (1965). His last name began with 'HA'; mine with 'HE'. Arthur remembered me & wrote me a letter, sending me a couple of old 8 x 10 glossies he had of himself from back then. It took me a few days to remember him, as our friendship had been that casual.

"At any rate, we began corresponding with one another, including Christmas cards. Both of us were in bad marriages then. He got divorced in 1993. I fled for my life from an abusive relationship & got divorced in '94. He began corresponding with me on a regular basis once I fled to Charleston, SC. He was very supportive of me.

"After a while we began to discover we had a LOT in common when it came to our mutual interests & general outlook on life. Not only did the letter writing increase, but we began calling each other on the phone. Soon our phone bills looked like the national debt!

"Arthur moved to Charleston in September of 1995 from Buffalo, NY. We were married on May 10, 1997."

Yes, I do miss her. She & I were a TEAM, something that was lacking in our respective previous marriages.

But life goes on.

Doing this book was a big help to me, as was all the warm support of family & friends.

Now this book is yours to peruse.

If you like it, tell your friends. If not, tell your enemies

TABLE OF CONTENTS

Educators

In Service to Our Country

T.V. & Radio

The World Stage

Authors & Writers

THE DAPPER GENTLEMAN

(Tony Bickley)

If you are fortunate enough to have the 33 & ⅓ LP record titled "A New Canaan Christmas Eve", you have a fine slice of local history.

On it is heard the annual non-denominational Christmas Eve service as delivered by the Rev. Loring D. Chase at the Congregational Church of New Canaan. The service took a half-hour, followed by a half-hour of Christmas caroling on God's Acre, a tradition which is still done each year. "Chuck" Chase repeated the service after the carol sing-along.

At the beginning of the recording are heard a pair of carols from God's Acre. Then the bells from the church begin to peal & the people begin entering the narthex, warmly greeted by then Sexton Wassily Bublick (pron. "Boob-lick"). One distinct voice is heard to say: "Thank you, same to you". The man uttering that response was Tony Bickley. (This was recorded just over 60 years ago.)

Tony was a very active member of that church. My parents & older brother were members of it; I was to become one in 1960.

Tony was a professional actor. Born in Philadelphia, he appeared in many TV shows. These included the anthology series "The Kraft Playhouse", "Robert Montgomery Presents", & "Studio One" back in the days of "live" TV drama. His stage credits included "Man & Superman", as well as "The Best Man".

He was not known to the general public, but that's one of the plusses of being a working actor rather than a "household name". Tony had an aura about him that projected sophistication. Indeed, he had good stage presence while off-stage. His voice was pleasant, but authoritative.

Tony & his family were very involved with the local "amateur" group, the Town Players. Actually the word amateur is a misnomer when it came to this theatrical group, as it had many current & past professional members. Yours truly was a rank amateur when I joined TP as a teenager. In addition to acting in plays I helped build flats in the barn on Tony's property, which served as a temporary storage area for TP.

Shortly after my discharge from the US Army I'd heard about a Burt Lancaster film that was shot in New Canaan & environs. The movie was "The Swimmer".

Tony was in the beginning of the film hosting some friends outdoors by poolside. Burt, clad only in swim trunks, announces to those assembled that he's going to swim home through all the pools in this town. Sound thrilling to you?

(Yawn.)

True, I haven't seen the movie since its debut, but frankly at that time I wasn't really impressed with it. Despite the movie's quasi "Twilight Zone" ending, I thought to myself who cares? I found nearly all of the film's characters to lack real depth. (Maybe Burt only swam in the shallow parts of the various pools.) But, as I stated earlier, I haven't seen the film in over 50 years. Perhaps a second viewing is called for.

Tony Bickley did some work on various "soaps" prior to passing away in 1976. He was 67 years old.

ANOTHER ACADEMY GUY

(Lee Bowman)

No, NOT West Point or any of the other service academies. Here I'm talking about one of my alma maters, the American Academy of Dramatic Arts. Lee went there as well, albeit many years before me.

Lee began his acting career as a handsome leading man, but he also became the fellow that lost the girl to another guy as time went on in his films. He was in movies from 1937 through 1964.

He portrayed the spoiled rich kid trying to get out of the US Army in the 1941 Abbott & Costello comedy, "Buck Privates", which was released during the peacetime draft days in the months prior to US entry into World War II. (The Andrews Sisters warbled "Boogie Woogie Bugle Boy from Company B" in that flick.)

Lee acted opposite some glamorous leading ladies during the heyday of his career in the 1940's. These included Rita Hayworth ("Cover Girl"); Susan Hayward ("Smash-Up: The Story of a Woman"); & Doris Day ("My Dream is Yours"). Alas, he lost Rita to Gene Kelly in "Cover Girl". In the film opposite Susan, he was the crooner married to an alcoholic singer. This was loosely based on the marriage that Bing Crosby & his first wife, Dixie Lee, had.

Lee was the first Ellery Queen on TV during the 1950's. He even hosted a TV game show entitled "What's Going On?"

He left the acting profession after 1968 & became involved with media training for the Republican party. Richard Nixon's administration hired Lee to help out freshman representatives with their voice delivery & staging, much as Robert Montgomery had done with President Dwight D. Eisenhower during the '50's. In fact, Lee was the emcee for both the 1968 & 1972 G.O.P. conventions.

Lee became Chairman of the Kinstree Group, which was a consulting firm that offered communication skills to business & politicians worldwide. He helped develop the conversational style of speaking for them, which is still in use by them in media matters today.

Lee Bowman died from a heart attack on Christmas Day in 1979. He was just 3 days shy of his 65th birthday.

THE GUMSHOE

(Lon Clark)

"This case has been a tough one. I got back to my office, both weary & tense from the day of frustration. I definitely needed a drink. I reached for the bottle inside my top desk drawer. I opened it & drained the contents. It was only ink, but hey, anything will do in a pinch."

The above dialogue was much like that found in paperbacks & pulp magazines about private eyes back in the middle decades of the 20th century. That was the heyday of that genre.

Lon Clark was, from 1943 till 1955, radio's "Nick Carter, Master Detective". His rich baritone voice was perfect for such a character. (This was broadcast over MBS, the long defunct Mutual Broadcasting System.)

Lon, his then wife, & two sons (Lon Jr & Steve) lived just two doors away from me in New Canaan. I remember that Lon instilled a love of music in his sons by sitting & listening to various LP's with them.

While Lon appeared on many network radio shows back in the 1940's & '50's, by late 1955 the glory days of radio had come to an end. Lon opted for both the Broadway & Off-Broadway stage. One of his most memorable stage roles came when he replaced Jason Robards in the role of Jamie in the Broadway production of Eugene O'Neill's "Long Day's Journey into Night" in 1956.

A native of Minnesota, he got his start doing radio drama in Cincinnati before relocating to New York. Lon Clark passed away in a Manhattan hospital at age 86 in 1998.

Oh, yes: One of the sponsors during the run of "Nick Carter" was Acme Products. They were manufacturer's of home improvement products such as Kem-Tone Paint & Lin-X, a floor cleaning wax. (They definitely were NOT the firm used to ship things to

Wile E. Coyote in his persistent, albeit vain, attempts to capture the Roadrunner in the Warner Brothers cartoons of yesteryear.)

"PLACES, PLEASE"

(Wendell Corey)

Memories of New Canaan: A note form Robin Corey Hollister

My family moved to New Canaan in the Fall of 1954. My father was then in the lead role of "The Night of the Auk" on Broadway. We moved to be closer to the city and because my parents, who grew up in New England, felt more comfortable there. In fact, they were happy to have the opportunity. So, we came from Beverley Hills to a wonderful house on Dan's Highway and became immediately enchanted. All my siblings will say that our times in New Canaan were among our happiest. We loved the change of seasons, the woods, the gentleness of the town. I was in the 5th grade and made two friends for life, Brooke Maddux and Cassia Besson. The next year we bought a house on St John's Place, where every day we explored the town on our bikes, before riding to the train station where we met our father at the end of the day. We loved life in New Canaan, quickly becoming comfortable with our special town. However, the nature of our father's work led us back to California in the winter of 1957, where my Dad began filming "Loving You" with Elvis Presley. As you might expect this was a very exciting time for us, but even so, I missed New Canaan and my best friends. In the time since, we have shared visits and events and to this day letters continue to pass between us. After many years living in California, New England still felt like home, and eventually I moved back again. In Massachusetts I raised my four children, became a Psychologist, and have spent my professional and family life just a little bit north of New Canaan.

Wendell Corey: A Biography

Actor Wendell Corey was a direct descendent of a 19th century Lowell, Massachusetts mill worker. Three Corey generations lived and worked in Lowell, the cradle of America's Industrial Revolution. His great-grandfather Alvin Corey came from Northern Vermont to work in the Merrimack Mills as a machinist in the mid-1800's. His grandfather, George Corey, used these skills to become an inventor. Wendell was the youngest of four siblings and born in Dracut, a small town adjacent to Lowell, on March 20, 1914. He later moved to Springfield, MA where his father was a paymaster and later a lay congregational minister. He graduated from Longmeadow High School. From his modest background he emerged to become an internationally recognized theatre, film and television star.

He began his professional career in 1938 touring New England in the play "I Want A Policeman", a production of the Federal Theatre Project – a program of the U.S. Government's Work Progress Administration (WPA). He became a member of the Copley Theatre Players, acting in Boston's old Copley Theatre. He performed there in such plays as "Goodbye Again" and "The Great American Family."

Soon, Wendell began to venture into other regional theatre and in 1942, he appeared with Gloria Swanson in "Reflected Glory" at the Maplewood Theatre in Maplewood, New Jersey. Now, Wendell was headed for Broadway. In 1943 he appeared in "The First Million" at the Ritz Theatre, the first of Wendell's fifteen Broadway shows. Following his critically acclaimed leading role in the 1945 Broadway production of Elmer Rice's "Dream Girl", Wendell was offered his first movie role in the Hal Wallis production "Desert Fury" with Burt Lancaster and Lizabeth Scott.

Shortly thereafter, Wendell signed his first multi-film contract and appeared as the leading man in three films with Barbara Stanwyck, "The File of Thelma Jordan", "The Furies", and "Sorry, Wrong Number." Now, a fast-rising Hollywood star, he was next paired with Joan Crawford as the romantic lead in "Harriet Craig." Over the next several years more than 25 movie roles would follow.

Wendell's first lead in a television series came when he played the harbormaster in "Harbor Command" on NBC. He later starred in "Peck's Bad Girl", "American Playhouse" and "The Eleventh Hour", a top-rated show of the mid 1960's. In it he played a psychiatrist – the first in prime-time television.

Wendell was a member of the Board of Governors of the Screen Actor's Guild for 16 years. He was a member of the Board of Governors of The Academy of Motion Picture Arts and Sciences for 10 years, serving as president for two of those years.

An actor's actor was how friends and colleagues described Wendell Corey and in 1958 he was honored with a Star on Hollywood Boulevard's famous Walk of Stars.

Even though he became an international figure, Wendell was first and always a family man. On November 9, 1938 he married Alice Wiley, at the time a fellow actress in Boston's Copley Theatre Players. Together they raised four children and continued to act in summer theaters whenever possible. The Corey family divided their time between East and West Coasts - with annual cross-country drives to the Berkshires in Massachusetts, home of Wendell's parents.

Wendell Corey died on November 8, 1968 and is buried with his parents and wife in the Berkshire town of Becket, Massachusetts. After Wendell's death, his wife Alice continued in community theater, directing and producing plays in Cottage Grove Oregon until her death on November 24, 2007. Their youngest daughter Bonnie passed away in 1999. Robin, Jonathan and Jennifer now live in cities throughout the United States.

Partial list of film credits:

Desert Fury	Jamaica Run
I Walk Alone	Laughing Ann
The Search	Hell's Half Acre
Sony, Wrong Number	Rear Window
Any Number Can Play	The Brave and The Bold
The Accused	The Big Knife
File of Thelma Jordan	The Killer Is Loose
No Sad Songs for Me	The Rack
Holiday Affair	The Rainmaker
The Furies	Loving You
My Man and I	The Light In The Forest
Carbine Williams	Alias Jesse James
Harriet Craig	he Wild North
The Great Missouri Raid	Rich, Young and Pretty

Partial list of actors with whom he worked in these films:

Burt Lancaster	Kirk Douglas
Grace Kelly	Katherine Hepburn
Robert Mitchum	Barbara Stanwyck
Joan Crawford	Paul Newman
James Stewart	Natalie Wood
Jessica Tandy	Raymond Burr
Elvis Presley	Carol Lynley
Ray Milland	Fess Parker

Thanks, Robin

Photo # 1 is on set of "Rear Window" with James Stewart,
Grace Kelly, & Wendell.

Photo # 2 is the Corey family at home on St. John's Place: (l to r) Alice, Jenny,
Bonnie (on Wendell's lap), Jonathan, & Robin.
(Pet dogs Rover & Christine are in front.)

"WHERE HAVE I SEEN THAT GUY?"

(Tony Goldwyn)

Jever go walking along some street & see a familiar face & asked yourself that question?

It might apply to Tony Goldwyn.

He was the friend that betrayed Patrick Swayze in the movie, "Ghost". He portrayed Colonel Bagley in "The Last Samurai". He performed the role of a fictitious U.S. President in the ABC TV drama, "Scandal".

These are just three of the many roles he has done. Tony is also a singer, director, & political activist. He also has followed in his family's footsteps by functioning as a producer.

Yes, THAT Goldwyn was Tony's grandfather, Samuel L. Goldwyn. Tony's father, Samuel Jr, was also a producer. The elder Samuel Goldwyn did change his last name. I'm sure that Tony might agree that the name Goldwyn looks far better on a marquee than old Samuel's original moniker of Goldfish.

Tony was born in Los Angeles in 1960. He is a graduate of both Brandeis University & the London Academy of Music & Dramatic Art. His role in "Ghost" was one of his earliest career efforts, but he also portrayed the HIV positive interior designer Kendall Dobbs on the TV sitcom, "Designing Women".

Tony has numerous New York theater credits on his resume, including a revival of the Broadway musical "Promises, Promises". He has also directed numerous TV shows, such as "Dexter"; "Grey's Anatomy"; & "Law & Order: Criminal Intent".

His TV credits are virtually as long as your arm. He has acted in such programs as "St. Elsewhere"; "Matlock"; "L.A. Law"; "Hunter"; the original edition of "Murphy Brown"; "Tales from the Crypt"; & "Frasier".

Tony, like another of that same first name earlier profiled (Tony Bickley) is a working actor. Indeed it must feel good, after a day performing, to say as the late Arthur Treacher once did on the "Merv Griffin Show" many years ago: "Say the words, get the money, & go home".

HERE'S YOUR EMCEE'

(Joel Grey)

Not too many actors can boast of winning both a Tony & an Oscar, but Joel Grey certainly can.

Joel resided in New Canaan around the time he played the Master of Ceremonies in the Broadway production of "Cabaret". (His daughter, actress Jennifer Grey, was a very young kid when they called New Canaan home.)

Joel was born in Cleveland, OH, in 1932. His father was Jewish comedian & musician Mickey Katz, who was a member of Spike Jones & His City Slickers back in the 1940's.

Joel decided early on to become an actor & he was a young talent selected by Eddie Cantor to appear on the "Colgate Comedy Hour" in 1951. After that he struggled for several years, getting small roles on such 1950's TV fare as "December Bride"; "Maverick"; "The Ann Sothern Show"; & "77 Sunset Strip". (On that last mentioned show I'm still trying to figure out what the character Kookie meant by calling a girl the "ginchiest".)

But it was on Broadway where his star really began to shine. He had juicy roles in "Come Blow Your Horn"; "Stop the World ~ I Want to Get Off", & "Half a Sixpence" before landing the part of the emcee in "Cabaret", for which he won a Tony. He also did the title role in "George M!" late in the 1960's. Years later he scored again in a revival of "Cabaret". He then went on to portray Amos Hart in the musical "Chicago" & The Wizard of Oz in "Wicked".

Joel has done many films, most notably "Cabaret" (for which he garnered an Academy Award for Best Supporting Actor); "The

Seven Percent Solution"; "Buffalo Bill & the Indians"; & the 1999 made-for-TV version of Dickens' "A Christmas Carol". (He portrayed the "Ghost of Christmas Past" in that last named film; Sir Patrick Stewart was Scrooge.)

Speaking of TV, he has a huge list he can put on his resume, with guest appearances on such programs as "Ironside"; "Night Gallery"; "The Carol Burnett Show"; "The Muppet Show"; "Dallas"; "Matlock"; "Star Trek: Voyager"; "Buffy, the Vampire Slayer"; "Touched by an Angel"; "Law & Order: Criminal Intent"; & (appropriately) "Grey's Anatomy".

The multi-talented Joel is an avid photographer & thus far has had four books of his photos published: "Pictures I Had to Take"; "Looking Hard at Unexpected Things"; "Images from My Phone" (his cell phone, no less); & "The Billboard Papers". The Museum of the City of New York had a 2011 exhibit of his photography entitled: "Joel Grey: A New York Life".

Though married for 24 years, he revealed in an interview with "People" magazine in 2015 that he is gay. His autobiography, "Master of Ceremonies", discusses that as well as his family life & career.

Jennifer & Joel Grey.

FROM CAPE CANAVERAL TO THE LONE STAR STATE

(Larry Hagman)

He could claim Nellie Forbush as his mother & Peter Pan as his "father".

Those were a pair of roles portrayed on Broadway by his real life mother, Mary Martin. Her son, Larry Hagman, decided to follow his mom's footsteps in a career in show business.

Larry is most famous for a pair of roles he played on TV: astronaut Tony Nelson on the 1960's sitcom, "I Dream of Jeannie", & (most famously) as the villainous J.R. Ewing on the prime time soap, "Dallas", many years later.

It seems apropo that he was born in Fort Worth, TX, in 1931. His mother split with his father when Larry was not quite five years old. His father wanted Larry to become a lawyer, which is what he was. But the "acting bug" bit the son.

He began acting professionally in 1950. He was even a member of the London production of "South Pacific" in which his mother starred there after she left the Broadway cast. But the Korean War was raging then & Larry enlisted in the US Air Force for a four year hitch in 1952. Following his discharge in 1956, he appeared in such TV series as "Sea Hunt" & in the films "Ensign Pulver" & "Fail-Safe".

Larry's big break occurred when he was cast opposite Barbara Eden in "I Dream of Jeannie" in 1965. That show lasted until 1970.

He worked as an actor pretty steadily after "Jeannie" wrapped. He did starring roles in a pair of shortlived shows in the early 1970's, but he did okay in supporting parts in films. Among his credits are "The Group"; "Harry & Tonto"; "Mother, Jugs, & Speed"; "In Harm's Way"; "The Eagle Has Landed"; "Superman: The Movie"; & "SOB".

Then he mosied on down to "Dallas".

Actually, he had the choice of starring in two TV series at the time: "The Waverly Wonders" or "Dallas". He wisely chose the latter, on which he became the villain you love to hate. "Texas tea" was the name of the game in that nighttime "soaper" & the character of J.R. Ewing was as unscrupulous as they come. The show became a mega-hit when it debuted in 1978. The producers decided to end the second season by having someone shoot Larry's character. The cliffhanger ending kept everybody abuzz that summer & well into fall with the question, "Who shot J.R.?"

So, who shot J.R.?

It took until the night of November 21, 1980, for it to be revealed. It was his sister-in-law, Kristen (portrayed by Bing's daughter, Mary Frances Crosby), who was just as selfish as J.R. Of course J.R. recovered & was in all 357 episodes of the series, which finally ended in 1991.

His career was given such a tremendous boost that Schlitz Beer even did a commercial that had Larry clad like J.R. An off-camera announcer said: "Refreshing Schlitz Beer...the gusto's back", after which Larry grinned & remarked: "...and I'm gonna get it!"

Larry in real life was known as a heavy drinker. He also enjoyed taking LSD & later switched from booze to marijuana. Larry said of pot: "I liked it because it was fun, it made me feel good, & I never had a hangover".

He & Carroll O'Connor were good friends since their struggling days as actors in New York. He offered moral support to Carroll following the death of his son, Hugh. Both father & son were in episodes of TV's "In the Heat of the Night", which Larry directed. Larry even delivered a eulogy at Carroll's funeral.

Larry married a Swedish woman, Maj Axelsson, in 1954. They stayed together until Larry predeceased her in 2012. Sadly she was diagnosed with Alzheimer's in 2008. He cared for her & put his acting chores on hiatus, but her condition worsened & by 2010 she needed round-the-clock care. (She passed away in 2016.)

Larry's own health went downhill as well. He was diagnosed with liver cancer in 1995, but was very fortunate to have a liver transplant shortly after the diagnosis was made. In 2011 he was diagnosed with stage 2 throat cancer. He had a tumor surgically removed from his tongue later that year. It was said to be the size of an acorn.

But acute myeloid leukemia caught up with Larry Hagman & he succumbed to that in November of 2012 in a hospital in (of all places) Dallas. Fellow "Dallas" co-stars Linda Gray & Patrick Duffy were at his bedside when he died.

"MONKEYS IS THE CWAZIEST PEOPLE"

(Lew Lehr)

The above quote was part of the shtick used by old time vaudevillian comic Lew Lehr. It was a popular catchphrase in its day.

Lew was born in Philadelphia in 1895. While he got his start on the vaudeville stage, it was in newsreels & short subjects where he gained the greatest fame.

He was the writer, editor, & commentator on the segment of Fox Movietone News that was titled "Dribble-Puss Parade". Whatever subject he covered in those old newsreels, he generally gave it a somewhat sardonic commentary, particularly when Fox Movietone inserted old Edison films into the newsreel mix. He did this for that newsreel company from 1932 until his death. His commentary was included on their newsreels (albeit posthumously) for several years after his passing.

He did other shorts (some 300 or so in all), such as "Adventures of a Newsreel Cameraman", "Lew Lehr's Unnatural History", "Magic Carpet", & "Tintypes". Starting in 1946 he did shorts titled "Drizzle-Puss Parade" for 20th Century Fox, which featured his jaded look at things saw in his journeys across the United States.

Lew began to appear on radio in the late 1930's, serving as one of the quizmasters on "Detect & Collect". He became a regular on the "Camel Comedy Caravan" & was a panelist on "Stop Me if You Heard This One". In fact he authored a book with the title of that last named show, as well as produced "Lew Lehr's Cookbook for Men", both of which came out in 1949. He was caricatured in numerous "Looney Tunes" of yore.

He resided late in his life on Ponus Ridge Road.. His daughter had her own radio show on WOR. Dana (NCHS'63), the late Darriell (NCHS '65), Josh ('67), & Jillisa Webster are his grandchildren.

Lew Lehr passed away in 1950 in Brookline, MA. He was only 54 years old.

"I'M FLYING!"

(Mary Martin)

Mary literally flew into television screens throughout the nation in March of 1955.

The program was "Peter Pan". Mary had been performing that on Broadway then. She was to do two more live performances on TV in subsequent years. It was but one of many highlights in a career in which she literally flew.

She was born in Weatherford, TX, in 1913. She was a good student, possessing a photographic memory which stood her in good stead in her show business career. She married Benjamin Hagman when she was just 17. (Son Larry came from that union.) While her mother approved of the marriage, her father did not. He thought she was too young to have gotten married & handled her divorce.

Mary was bored in marriage anyway, being the creative person that she was. She ditched Texas to try her luck as an actress in Hollywood, leaving little Larry behind. She found work here & there, but then moved east where she was cast in a musical called "Leave It to Me!", penned by Cole Porter. Though only having a supporting role in it, she got her big break by singing the song, "My Heart Belongs to Daddy", in that 1938 production.

She tried Hollywood again after that triumph, but most of her films were forgettable. Thus she returned to Broadway & was cast in the Kurt Weill musical, "One Touch of Venus", in 1943. She did other minor successes after that before auditioning for the lead role in "Kiss Me Kate". But Mary turned doing that show down in favor of portraying Nellie Forbush is Rodgers & Hammerstein's "South Pacific". (The rest, as they say, is history.)

Mary landed on TV in June of 1953, doing a memorable duet with Ethel Merman on the "Ford 50th Anniversary Show", simulcast on both CBS & NBC. The two Broadway stars sang many of their show tunes while seated on swivel stools next to each other. It made for not only a memorable performance by the two ladies, but set the standard for many others that later did the same thing on other variety shows & specials.

Mary won both a Tony & a pair of Emmys for playing "Peter Pan". She also garnered Tony Awards for both "South Pacific" & "The Sound of Music" in which she was cast as Maria Von Trapp.

The so-called Golden Age of Broadway faded away after the mid-1960's. So, too, did Mary's career. She had married Richard Halliday, a drama critic for the long gone "New York World Telegram & Sun" before taking a position as movie critic with the "New York Daily News". The couple settled in Brazil, where Halliday died in 1973.

Mary Martin passed away in California in 1990.

*Mary Martin "kinda/sorta" flying in the "Honey Bun" number
from the London production of "South Pacific".*

A WOLF CAME HOWLING

(Christopher Meloni)

In this case it was a Wolf named Dick, the producer of the various "Law & Order" TV series.

When I think of Christopher, I think of his role as Elliot Stabler in "Law & Order SVU". He portrayed the perpetually angry Elliot for a dozen seasons (1999-2011).

Christopher was born in Washington, DC, in April of 1961. He graduated the University of Colorado at Boulder, majoring in history. However, he also studied drama there & the "acting bug" obviously bit him. He subsequently studied acting under Sanford Meisner at the Neighborhood Playhouse in New York.

He paid his dues, landing small roles in assorted movies & TV shows until HBO's "Oz" beckoned in 1998 & "SVU" did so the following year. He played on both series simultaneously until exiting "Oz" in 2003.

"SVU" is a well-cast show. His co-partner in crime fighting on that show was Mariska Hargitay, the daughter of the late Jayne Mansfield. Both teamed up well in their roles. In fact, she became godmother to Christopher's daughter in real life.

But a contract squabble ended Christopher's association with "SVU" in May, 2011. Thus, he left the show.

Christopher had done movies prior to "SVU", such as "12 Monkeys" & "Runaway Bride". He did "Wet Hot American Summer" & "Harold & Kumar Go to White Castle" while on "SVU", then performed in "Man of Steel" & "42" after leaving that show. (In "42" he portrayed Brooklyn Dodger manager Leo Durocher.) He's done several TV shows since then as well.

"YA, YENNY"

(Rosemary Rice)

"(I remember) the house on Steiner Street where I was born....And I remember my family as we were then: My brother Nels, my little sister Dagmar, and, of course, Papa. But most of all I remember Mama."

Those words were spoken weekly at the beginning of the old TV show "Mama". They were usually uttered as she leafed through an old photo album. Actress Rosemary Rice portrayed the oldest daughter, Katrin, on that series.

Rosemary lived a pretty anonymous life, even though she was a working actress. In fact I surprised several friends from New Canaan that are about my age by informing them that she did indeed call it home for most of her adult life.

"Mama" was a sentimental show set in the San Francisco of the early 20th century. It dealt with the lives of the Hansen family, the parents being Norwegian immigrants. The half-hour CBS program was billed as a family comedy, but it certainly had pathos as well. It was on the air from 1949 till 1957.

The title role was given to veteran star Peggy Wood. Judson Laire made a fine Papa, while Dick Van Patten was Nels & future feminist pioneer Robin Morgan portrayed Dagmar. (The title above refers to how Mama oft times answered her best friend, Jenny.) The show was broadcast "live" weekly from a studio above the Oyster Bar in New York's Grand Central Terminal.

Rosemary said the cast were very close to each other. In fact, she affectionately referred to Judson Laire as "Papa" until his 1979 passing.

Sadly, most of the old kinescopes of that program no longer exist. Fortunately, Rosemary held on to some of them & eventually donated them to the Paley Center for Media (nee the Museum of Broadcasting). A few of them can be viewed on Youtube.

Rosemary did other TV work, appearing in the anthology series "Kraft Television Theatre" & "Playhouse 90", as well as such soaps as "The Edge of Night", "One Life to Live", & "Search for Tomorrow". She also wrote, narrated, & sang on 15 children's record albums

She did voiceovers as well. Do you remember hearing this on both TV & radio years ago for Clairol? On it one heard a female voice say: "If I've only one life to live, let me live it as a blonde". That was Rosemary's voice. (She also provided the voice for the Bell Telephone exhibit at the 1964/'65 New York World's Fair.)

Rosemary Rice (who hailed originally from Montclair, NJ,) passed away in Stamford, CT, at age 87 in 2012.

Cast of "Mama": (l to r) Judson Laire, Dick Van Patten,
Peggy Wood, Robin Morgan, & Rosemary Rice.

NO LONGER AN ITEM (1)

(Tim Robbins)

Tim Robbins probably would have liked my posting on my Facebook page on Veterans Day, 2018: "Happy Veterans Day to all who served....And to think that 100 years ago today, the 'war to end all wars' ended in an armistice. As the song sez: 'When will they ever learn? When will they ever learn?'"

(The words quoted in the above song are from "Where Have All the Flowers Gone?", by the late Pete Seeger.)

Before any of you readers go thinking that this author was a flag burning draft dodger, I will state that I am a combat veteran of Vietnam (US Army's 25th Infantry Division, 1966-'67), In other words, I've been there & done that.

Both Tim & his former long time "POSSLQ" (Susan Sarandon) are on the same wave length when it came to political activism. Both were opposed to the pre-emptory invasion of Iraq in 2003, as were my my late wife & myself. (BTW, a "POSSLQ" is a "Person of the Opposite Sex Sharing Living Quarters", according to some US government bureaucracy during the 1980's.)

Tim is well known as an actor, but he's also a director, producer, screenwriter, & musician. His most famous acting roles are in the films "Bull Durham", "Jacob's Ladder", "Mystic River" & "The Shawshank Redemption". He directed both "Bob Roberts" & "Dead Man Walking".

Tim was born in West Covina, CA, in 1958 but was raised primarily in New York City. His father, who at one time managed the Gaslight Café in Greenwich Village, was a member of the folk singing group, the Highwaymen ("Michael" & "Cotton Fields"). Tim is a 1981 graduate of the UCLA Film School. He paid his dues by landing small parts in both TV's "Moonlighting" & "St. Elsewhere", as well as the film, "Top Gun", He got his big break in "Bull Durham", where he met co-star Susan Sarandon.

Tim received an Oscar as Best Supporting Actor for his role in 2003's "Mystic River". At 6'5" it is said he is the tallest actor to ever receive an Academy Award. (He was also nominated as Best Director for 1995's "Dead Man Walking".)

He & Ms Sarandon lived together from 1988 thru 2009. Their union produced two sons.

Tim Robbins now makes his home in Pound Ridge, NY.

NO LONGER AN ITEM (II)

(Susan Sarandon)

Susan was born Susan Tomalin in Queens in 1946, and was raised in Edison, NJ. She majored in Drama at The Catholic University of America, from which she earned a BA in 1968.

Her acting career really got going when she was cast as a troubled teen in the 1970 movie, "Joe". I first remember seeing her cast as Jack Lemmon's fiancé in the 1974 re-make of the Ben Hecht-Charles MacArthur classic, "The Front Page". (I thought at the time that Hildy Johnson, portrayed by then 49 year old Jack Lemmon, was robbing the cradle with Peggy, Susan's character in that film.) Overall it was a pretty good movie.

Susan was married at that time to Chris Sarandon, who was struggling in his acting career. They met in college & were divorced in 1979.

I'm probably one of the few people on the planet that has never seen "The Rocky Horror Picture Show", in which Susan had the lead role of Janet. Later that year (1975) she was opposite Robert Redford in "The Great Waldo Pepper". She later did "Pretty Baby", "Atlantic City", & "The Witches of Eastwick". But her major breakthrough came in 1988's "Bull Durham", which was where she met Tim Robbins. The two fell in love lived together for 21 years, part of that in New Canaan.

Onward & upward progressed Susan's career. "Thelma & Louise" was the epitome of a "chick flick" at the time of its 1991 release. She garnered an Oscar as Best Actress in "Dead Man Walking", which Robbins directed. She has made many other films since then.

Susan is very much the activist. She was appointed as the Goodwill Ambassador for UNICEF in 1999. She was one of eight women chosen to carry the Olympic Flag during opening ceremonies for the Winter Games in Turin, Italy, in 2006.

On the political front, she & Robbins supported Ralph Nader's bid for the presidency in 2000. Both Susan & Tim were very much opposed to the pre-emptive war in Iraq, which the George W. Bush administration began in 2003. This further alienated her from her mother, a solid Republican who backed that controversial war.

In 2008 she & Robbins campaigned for John Edwards in his failed bid for the Democratic presidential nomination. She wholeheartedly threw her support behind Sen. Bernie Sanders in his quest for the 2016 nomination that Hillary Clinton eventually won. She didn't like either Donald Trump or Mrs Clinton for that office, so she backed Jill Stein, the Green Party candidate, late in the election cycle.

Susan Sarandon continues being politically active. She & Robbins went to "Splitsville" in 2009, but both live now in Pound Ridge, NY (albeit in separate places).

Agree with her or not, Susan does have the right to protest. After all, this is still a free country the last time I checked.

A ONE WOMAN REPERTORY COMPANY

(Cornelia Otis Skinner)

Cornelia was born to a theatrical family. Her father was Otis Skinner, a noted stage actor of the late 19th & early 20th century. Her mother, Maud Durbin, was an actress in many of his plays.

She was born in Chicago in 1899 & attended Bryn Mawr College. She studied theatre at the Sorbonne in Paris.

Cornelia first gained fame by portraying a variety of parts in such one woman dramas as "The Empress Eugenie", "The Loves of Charles II", "Mansions on the Hudson", & "The Wives of Henry VIII" during the 1930's. She also appeared in numerous plays (albeit with other actors & actresses), such as in "Major Barbara" & "The Searching Wind", among others. She was well received for her light-hearted performances & her razor sharp wit.

She was a very versatile person, as she wrote biographies of actress Sarah Bernhardt ("Madame Sarah") & playwrights Howard Lindsay & Russell Crouse ("Life with Lindsay & Crouse"). One of her most famous books was "Our Hearts Were Young & Gay", which was co-written by Emily Kimbrough after they toured Europe following their college years. (This last book was made into a movie in 1944, which starred Gail Russell as Cornelia & Diana Lynn portraying Emily.)

Cornelia also co-wrote a play, "The Pleasure of His Company" (1958). Three years later this light-hearted comedy was made into a movie that starred Fred Astaire, Lilli Palmer, & Debbie Reynolds.

She was married to Alden S. Blodget & they had one son. She was also a member of the Colony Club in New York. The building

where that women's club was located was designed by famed architect: Stanford White & has been home to the American Academy
of Dramatic Arts since 1964.

Cornelia Otis Skinner passed away in 1979.

That's Emily Kimbrough on the left with Cornelia Otis Skinner.

THE FLIPPANT WISE GUY

(Arnold Stang)

Back when I was in my formative years in New Canaan, I got quite choosy about what comedians I truly liked on the new medium of Television. Jack Benny was certainly a favorite, as were Burns & Allen, Bob Hope, Danny Kaye, Martin & Lewis, & a young Carol Burnett.

There were those as well that I never found funny. That guy dressed as a clown that kept loading & unloading bananas while humming a tuneless tune comes to mind.

Then there were those who were more on the obnoxious side, such as Jack E. Leonard, Phil Silvers, & Arnold Stang. They just weren't my cup of tea.

But I'm entitled to my opinion & you to yours.

Arnold's shtick was the brash, street smart guy that berated others, most notably Milton Berle on the latter's TV show. He did other variety shows as well.

Arnold was born in New York City in 1918, although he did insist he hailed from Chelsea. MA. (Why that was, I don't know.) He got his start on radio in the 1940's portraying Seymour on "The Goldbergs". Comedian Henry Morgan employed him as his side-kick on his radio show, starting in 1946. Arnold portrayed Jughead on the radio show about comic book teen Archie Andrews.

He also had supporting roles in such films as "The Man with the Golden Arm" (1955) & "It's a Mad, Mad, Mad, Mad World" (1963). He & fellow comedian Marvin Kaplan played the attendants at the gas station that Jonathan Winters destroyed in the latter movie.

He was a working actor. He voiced the title role of "Top Cat" in the animated Hanna-Barbera TV series in the early 1960's. He was the television spokesman for the Chunky candy bar, in which he uttered the famous line: "Chunky, what a chunk of chocolate!".

Arnold did many other voiceovers in subsequent years. He talked to Pikachu in the animated "Hey You, Pikachu!"

Arnold Stang died in Newton, MA, in 2009 at age 91.

HEY, "I'M FLYING" AS WELL!

(Allison Williams)

Just like Mary Martin did during the 1950's, so did Allison Williams. She, too, flew into our television screens.

Allison is the daughter of former NBC News anchor (& present day same thing on MSNBC) Brian Williams. But she's made a name for herself in her own right.

Allison was born in 1988. She went to New Canaan's Country Day School, then left for Greenwich Academy. She is a graduate of Yale.

It didn't take her long to find employment in show biz, as she was cast as Marnie Michaels in the HBO comedy/drama series, "Girls", in 2012. In December of 2014 she was in the "live" TV production of "Peter Pan", with Christopher Walken taking on the role of Captain Hook, which Cyril Ritchard did opposite Mary Martin 60 years previously. (My late wife, Nan, & I saw Allison's portrayal of Peter Pan & we both thought she did a fine job.)

Allison also won acclaim in the horror film, "Get Out", in 2017. So, her star is ascending.

She married Ricky Van Veen that same year. They reside in Chelsea in Dutchess County, NY.

HE PUT A STAMP ON THE ART WORLD

(Walter DuBois Richards)

Pictured above is a lithograph of God's Acre, with the Congregational Church centered on top. This was done by Walter DuBois Richards.

Walter was known pretty much for his commercial art work that adorned many periodicals during their 20th century heyday. He drew ads for Cadillac & Ford, among others.

He was born on a farm in Ohio in 1907. He liked depicting hard working people in his art. Most of what he drew was in black & white. He liked the mundane, often instilling his drawings with strong dramatic contrasts. Some felt there was an air of mystery about his artwork.

Later in his career he designed 37 US postage stamps. These included prominent Americans; the Bald Eagle; the Beautification of America; conservation & the environment; the Giant Sequoias,; The Virginia Rotunda; the Boston State House; the Biltmore in

Asheville; Frank Lloyd Wright's Fallingwater; & Dulles Airport. These were done from 1967 through 1987.

Walter DuBois Richards passed away in New Canaan in 2006 at age 99.

LE PETIT DYNAMO

(Karen Santry)

Frisky is a good adjective to describe Karen Santry in the composition of her personality. She is indeed a very energetic woman that also possesses a great deal of charm.

She had the nickname of "Frisky" when she was a kid growing up in New Canaan. I first met her when I was a senior at NCHS & she was a freshman. Both she & the late Penny Austin were two of my "faves" in the NCHS class of '66 (a class loaded with LOTS of pretty girls, I might add).

Karen was born in Frankfurt am Main, Germany, in 1948. She lived there & in Holland before her parents settled in New Canaan when she was still very young. But it was in the Netherlands that she saw the works of Rembrandt as well as Vermeer & she got hooked on art.

She went on to earn a BS in Painting from Skidmore College in 1970 & an MFA in both Painting & Drawing at the University of Pennsylvania in 1974. Straight out of Skidmore she was employed by the Atlas Scenic Studios in Norwalk, CT. There she got her start painting scenery for the Broadway productions of "Hair" & "Jesus Christ Superstar". She said of that experience it "allowed me to think big & paint large". She had to work on scaffolding to do some of this work, but thankfully she has no fear of heights. This experience enabled her to work with Darla Olson Preservation in decorative painting at the White House in Al Gore's office and numerous other churches and capitols.

It was at Skidmore where she met the late Andy Warhol, who taught her printmaking. While at the University of Pennsylvania she did a series of portraits of David Bowie while he performed at the Tower Theatre. Thirty years later she did fashion illustration for designer Andre Van Pier and did a portrait of David Bowie in

Andre's leather jacket as well as the inaugural portraits of Laura Bush and her daughters in Andre's dresses.

Having moved to South Norwalk after Penn to be near Atlas Scenic studios she named the Art Community she promoted in South Norwalk SoNo!

She taught drawing for two years at Yale University while also teaching at the Silvermine guild of Art, but wanted to be closer to the bustling art world of Manhattan. She was also fascinated with the Haute-Couture evening ware. An artist named Janis Salek & she are the only two artists that have permission to draw the designers and runway models sponsored by Mercedes Benz during Fashion Week in New York City.

Karen has been as an Associate Professor of Art at the Fashion Institute of Technology in Manhattan since 1980. Not one to let the grass grow from the pavement of that borough, she has done painting for such diverse accounts as the Ballet Etudes; such book publishers as Bantam, Harper Collins, Penguin, Random House, & St. Martin's Press; CBS; Mercedes-Benz; the Metropolitan Opera; the New York Ballet; Nokia; Pfizer; "Psychology Today"; the Smithsonian; Sony Records; "Wedding Magazine"; Westinghouse; & the Westport Playhouse, among many others.

In 1999 Karen was one of five co-founders of Fashion Art Bank, Inc., in which she still remains very active. They are billed as the world's largest licensing company for Fashion Illustration. She believes that "art & fashion feed into each other".

Her late mother, Marcine, encouraged her to try and find an apartment in Westbeth, an artists' residence in the westernmost part of Greenwich Village, overlooking the Hudson River. (This is the old Bell Labs facility.) Currently she is painting larger than life size

Kabuki Cutouts. She has been living there for nearly 30 years in an apartment, which is both high & narrow and has a separate loft studio facing the Hudson River in Westbeth's I building. She says that when Westbeth began, it was with intent of having artists live there "to get a start on their art careers & then move out after four or five years". She quickly adds that "No one ever leaves". (That's because the rents are so low in this non-profit, art grant subsidized accommodation.) She says of her Westbeth neighbors: "Each artist is an inspiration. You see them coming from the opera or going to the ballet to perform ~~~ or taking a painting to the Whitney".

Sadly, all that art work in her basement studio (she resides on an upper floor) was ruined by the floodwaters of the Hudson created by the infamous Hurricane Sandy. This proved very costly to Karen, both artistically & financially. But Karen is a game gal that doesn't give up all that easily. Her fine art paintings and drawing have been shown in over 200 galleries nationally and internationally and her dream is to be included in the Whitney Biennial! Her website is www.karensantry.com

One of her colleagues in the Fashion Art Bank, Ms Marsha Silvestri, has this to say about Karen Santry: "(She) gives her all when she teaches. She addresses her students (as) 'Artists!', which puts them in the proper mindset for their life's work. She goes above & beyond in the classroom, creating an exciting visual environment for aspirants....Always respectful of individual talents, she draws the best out of people while pushing them to achieve more than what they expected of themselves....

"As a friend she is extremely kind, helpful, thoughtful, gener-ous, positive, fun, intelligent, interesting, loyal, (&) beautiful....(She has) high style dramatic flair & an energetic dynamic personality.

She's also quite humble regarding her own outstanding achievements & impressive credentials."

Ms Silvestri concludes by saying that "I also consider her a dear & trusted friend".

Second that motion, Ms Silvestri!

Karen's "pad" in The Village.
Samples of her artwork adorn both the left & right walls.

A SOCIAL COMMENTATOR AT THE
DRAWING BOARD

(Charles Saxon)

The above drawing appeared on the cover of the December 19, 1959, issue of *The New Yorker*. For those of you not in the know, that is the train station in New Canaan. This was drawn by Charles Saxon. (Cover courtesy of Conde Nast Publishing Company.)

Charles made his home in the Silvermine section of New Canaan near the border with neighboring Norwalk. One of his longtime friends & neighbors there was social critic & writer Vance Packard. Both men had much in common, but expressed themselves in different ways.

Whereas Packard wrote such social commontery books as "The Hidden Persuaders" & "The Status Seekers", Charles did his work via art. I well remember seeing his cartoons in *The New Yorker & The Saturday Evening Post*. His targets were typically the world of big business & suburban life. Packard said of him: "His main interest was in the lifestyles of the presumably sophisticated, and he saw himself as an interpreter of their world".

Lee Lorenz, his art editor at *The New Yorker* said of Charles' art work: "These people out in suburbia are easy targets for humor.... Seen as a whole, his work constitutes a unique social history of our time".

Saxon's barbs were razor sharp. An example of his commentary of the world of big business is contained in a 1984 cartoon from the abovementioned publication. The board chairman is depicted addressing his executives with the caption: "Of course, honesty is one of the better policies".

Charles was born in Brooklyn in 1920. He worked at both the satirical magazine *Ballyhoo* & Dell Publishing prior to World War II military service. As a pilot in the U.S. Army Air Corps, he led missions over Germany. He worked for Dell after the war, but also became a free-lance cartoonist.

He became a full-time cartoonist in 1955, joining the staff of *The New Yorker* the following year. He drew 92 covers for that magazine, as well as over 700 cartoons. His art work is available in a trio of books: "Oh, Happy Happy Happy"; "One Man's Fancy"; & "Honesty Is One of the Better Policies". He also did art in magazine ads for American Airlines, Bankers Trust, Chivas Regal, I.B.M., Mobil Oil, United Airlines, & Xerox, among other companies. He was also the recipient of a gold medal from the Art Directors Club & a Ruben Award from the National Cartoonists Society.

Charles Saxon passed away from heart failure in December, 1988. He maintained his sense of humor to the end, quipping to the paramedics that carried him out of his house: "I guess I'd better die; I just broke our best lamp".

Mr. & Mrs. Charles Saxon hosting a cocktail party

"WOULD YOU LIKE TO RIDE IN MY BEAUTIFUL BALLOON?"

(Lorna VanParys-Fisher)

"The above title is from, "Up, Up, and Away", penned in 1967 by Jimmy Webb & made famous by the 5th Dimension.

Actually, Lorna is a twin. Let's turn back the clock again to the 1960's for this comedic bit by Marty Allen & Steve Rossi:

ALLEN: "My wife's a twin."

ROSSI: "How do you tell them apart?"

ALLEN: "Her brother's taller."

Lorna has a twin SISTER named Helen, who is profiled under the category "WRITERS" in this book. They were born in New York City in May, 1945, but grew up in New Canaan, where she said: "We had a blast & were happy girls!"

The duo did attend New Canaan public schools through their freshman year at NCHS, then Lorna went away to Andover (nee Abbott) Academy in MA. She sez she hated prep school. She always seemed happy to be back home in New Canaan during holidays, as I used to run into her at the Congregational Church in town.

Lorna met her first husband, Art Daily, while attending NYU. They transferred out to the University of Colorado, where he earned a law degree. Lorna had a dual major in Fine Arts & Poli Sci. (That's Political Science on the latter, for those of you taking notes.)

Art got a position with Holland & Hart, a major Denver law firm, after graduation. They soon moved to Aspen. Their daughter, Piper, was born in 1971. The marriage didn't work out, but they parted amicably.

After the divorce Lorna & Piper began sailing on an antique yacht in the Caribbean & the west coast of Central America. They returned to Aspen for Piper's schooling, but they had some interesting adventures during their sailing excursions. These included (as

Lorna put it): "the use of cannabis; the violent storms; the silent coves laced with palm trees; floating in the limpid water; hidden rum distilleries among the palm trees"; etc.

Lorna lived in Aspen for 28 years. She managed a restaurant there & that's where she met some people that got her into the hot air balloon business. She started out as a crew member on the balloons & then took piloting lessons. She soon founded Aspen Balloon Adventure & received sponsorship from Absolute Vodka, who displayed their liquor logo on the envelope (a.k.a. colored fabric) of the balloon itself. She eventually became the first person to fly a hot air balloon over the Rockies, which included the highest point (Mount Elbert) of that mountain range.

Her ballooning adventures attracted the attention of a man named Guy VanParys, whom she described as "a debonair Belgian". He invited her to fly in competition over in Switzerland. Guy had a chalet there. They soon fell in love & got married, making their permanent residence in Belgium.

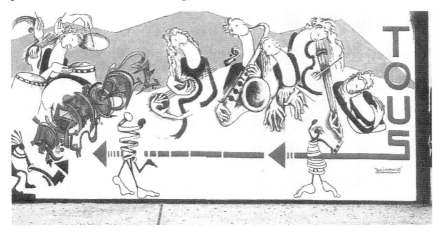

Lorna flew in Swiss balloon competition for 14 years. She had to have a co-pilot on flights over the Alps, but together she & her co-pilot set a record by flying over the Alps all the way to southern

Italy. However, the judges of that competition refused to recognize their flight record, for some unknown reason. (She eventually tired of that competition & instead began flying tourists in her hot air balloon for another 10 years.)

While in Belgium she began studying art under Francoise Andre. Ms Andre taught her the classical painting style of the old masters. She also learned how to converse in French fluently.

She & Guy moved to southern France after he sold his business. (He was a Belgian chocolateer.) Sadly, he passed away in 2008.

Lorna decided to handle her grief by climbing Africa's Mount Kilimanjaro. There she met Dr. Jean-Francois Fara & the two fell in love. Lorna even commuted between France & Vermont for 2 years, as she earned her MFA at Chicago university of Vermont College. She is now qualified to teach art at the university level.

She began shifting away from classical painting & her art work became more modern. A series of her paintings, "Moontide", is still on display in Tokyo, Paris, & New York City.

Lorna's art work even made it to the prestigious Salon d'Automne on the Champs Elysees in Paris. She is still very much involved in her art work, maintaining another studio in the Bushwick section of Brooklyn. She inherited a small Manhattan apartment from Guy & spends about 2 months of the year stateside.

Lorna VanParys-Fisher sums everything up as follows: "I am grateful for this passion I have for art. It will sustain me through the challenge of my advancing age". She admits that she's "had an unusual life, but each part brought me wonderful learning, dynamic experiences, & diverse friends".

"ARS GRATIA ARTIS"

(Claire Watson Garcia)

That old Latin motto used by MGM certainly applies to Claire Watson Garcia.

Claire has been an instructor at the prestigious Silvermine Guild of Artists in New Canaan for over 20 years. She runs workshops & courses in drawing & painting for the "absolute & utter beginner".

Claire's family moved to New Canaan from Eastchester, NY, when she was ten years old. She grew up in the Wahackme Road/ Ponus Ridge section of town. She was fascinated by the modern houses nearby to her family's home that had been designed by the famed "Harvard Five" architects.

Early on her parents enrolled her at the Silvermine Guild. She took to the art world like a duck takes to water. She had much support for her artistic endeavors from her family, her neighbors, & her teachers in the New Canaan Public Schools. She mentions such art teachers at NCHS as Alois Fabry, Bernice Hall, & Al Jacobsen as being most influential to her. She felt likewise about the late Nancy Hugo, then a recent Radcliffe graduate, who taught her English at NCHS. Claire stated that she treated the journals she assigned her students as if they "were written by Henry David Thoreau". She was most appreciative to Warren Allen Smith for teaching her how to write a coherent essay.

Claire was certainly active in the art world of NCHS. She was the literary editor of *The Spectator*. The staff of that in-school magazine for budding writers even put together a book. She also got into designing sets for our class plays.

She was the recipient of both an English & an Art award upon her 1963 graduation. This cemented her choice to continue pursuing both fields in life.

Claire went to Smith College for 2 & ½ years, but then transferred to UC Berkeley. She graduated from the latter with a Bachelors in Fine Arts in 1967. She heard Mario Savio speak from the steps of Sproul Hall at Berkeley. She also saw Grace Slick & the Jefferson Airplane at the legendary Fillmore.

It was at Berkeley that she met Baxter Garcia, who was to become her husband. Both were fellow students there & both were political activists against the controversial war in Vietnam. The Johnson administration was looking to draft any able bodied young man back then, so Claire & Baxter decided to relocate to Canada, where Baxter pursued his graduate degree. They stopped off at Claire's parents' house in New Canaan & got married in it just before trekking to "The Great White North". The FBI came calling at the Watson home in New Canaan in search of Baxter, but Claire's mom politely declined to tell them of their whereabouts.

Claire admits "it was a wrenching thing for us to leave the United States", but both fell in love with Toronto. Claire hooked on with some female American expats that were into the art scene. She said "they had a unique focus on inclusivity,...(which was) a novel concept...in the '70's....All the projects were guided by the desire to put into practice the notion that all people are created equal, and have a right to pursue their interests and find joy in them".

While in Toronto she helped develop Creating Together, which she says was "the first arts-oriented program for parents &

preschoolers". She also worked on Kids Can Press, "a groundbreaking children's book press with a socially progressive mandate". With the latter she illustrated Rosemary Allison's "Green Harpy at the Corner Store" in 1976. She both wrote & illustrated "Harriet and the Great Bike Robbery" in 1973 & "The Peanut Plan" in 1975. Claire also illustrated "The Women's Kit", which she said was the first multi-media educational package on gender for both middle & high school students.

Claire gave birth to their daughter, Elizbeth, in Toronto in 1977. She is a dual citizen & is married to actor Joshua Harto. She is now an established writer for both TV & films. She & Joshua have two children, Wilder & Augie.

The Carter administration pardoned all those "draft dodgers" that fled the US during Vietnam. Thus, Claire & Baxter returned to this country. They initially settled in Lynchburg, VA, but soon welcomed Baxter's landing a position shortly afterward that took them to Ridgefield, CT. That's when Claire literally began trodding the boards she did as a kid at the Silvermine Guild.

She authored a pair of books: "Drawing for the Absolute Beginner" (2003) & "Painting For the Absolute Beginner" (2009). (The former was revised in 2018 under the title "Drawing for The Absolute & Utter Beginner, Revised".)

She attended the 50th reunion of our class (NCHS '63) in October, 2013. Many attending it remarked that she looked as if she stepped out of the pages of our senior yearbook. You can see for yourself how little Claire Watson Garcia seems to have aged in the photo on the next page, which was taken at an NCHS "mini-reunion" at Cherry Street East in May, 2018.

(Please don't tell us you have a picture in the attic, Claire ~~~

LOL!)

Lunching at Cherry Street East are (l to r) Nancy (Hutchinson) Erdmann, Larry Creedon, Claire Watson Garcia, & Mike McKee. (May, 2018.)

Drawing for the

Absolute and Utter

Beginner

REVISED

15th Anniversary Edition

CLAIRE WATSON GARCIA

THIS AIN'T LEGALESE

(Raymond T. Benedict)

Somehow I cannot picture Raymond Terrell Benedict doing TV ads plugging his law firm with, say, a Greek Chorus or some such nonsense. ("If you've been in wrecks like Oedipus Rex...") He was much too classy for that. Besides, he didn't practice that type of law.

Ray was born in Norwalk in 1916. Sadly, his father died in 1921. His mother moved them to the Ridgefield CT/Lewisboro NY neck of the woods. He was exposed to the great outdoors there & this began his lifelong interest in both nature & conservation.

He graduated from Trinity Pauling School in Pauling, NY, in 1934, & then went on to Harvard. He became part of their championship swimming team there. He went on to get his law degree at Harvard Law School in 1941.

He fell in love & wed Jean Fulton in Chicago less than a fortnight after Pearl Harbor. He went in the US Navy soon after that, being onboard ship during the battles of Kwajalein, Eniwetok, Saipan, Tinan, & Leyte Gulf. He did distinguish himself during his wartime service.

Their eldest son, Henry, was born in July of 1945 while his dad was in the Pacific Theater. They would have two more children: Margaret (a.k.a. Teri), born in 11/46, & Charlie in 1/49. Ray worked in a small law firm in Norwalk until he got a big break in 1951.

That was the year when the prominent law firm of Cummings & Lockwood hired him to head their real estate department. Cummings & Lockwood were located then at 1 Atlantic Street in what was then the tallest building in Stamford. They are still in business today, but have since moved.

Ray had much to do with the founding of the Stamford Museum & Nature Center in 1955. He did likewise for the Country Club of Darien & the 900 acre Mianus River Gorge Reserve, which is in Bedford, NY. He also represented many large companies that relocated their corporate headquarters from New York City to Stamford years later.

Ray was but 43 years old when he argued before the US Supreme Court in 1959 in the case of John L. Senior v the Zoning Commission of New Canaan. He did so again there in 1963 with Fahy v Connecticut. (Both cases were heard when Earl Warren was Chief Justice.)

Ray also served on some corporate board of directors, most notably Central Hudson Gas & Electric. (They're based in Ellenville, NY.)

He & Jean purchased a 30 acre property (with the assistance of local realtor Mabel Lamb) at 8 Ponus Ridge Road in 1959, which was right on the New Canaan & Stamford town lines. The property had once been the summer residence of a Broadway producer of yore. Much renovation was needed, but the property consisted not only of a fairly large house, but a commercial greenhouse, a man made swimming pool with cabana, a clay tennis court, a 2-stall horse barn, & a tobacco curing room, among other amenities.

The family stayed there until Teri's sudden death in 1974. By then both sons were on their own, so they moved back to Norwalk. Raymond T. Benedict passed away in February of 1995, while Jean joined him in January of 2011. Henry told me his parents both died in the same bed they'd owned their entire married life.

A VERY SPECIAL LADY

(Nancy Blair)

1961 NCHS Yearbook Portrait

I first saw Ms Blair one Sunday morning when she was walking across Church Street to get to Sunday morning worship at the old Methodist Church. I was probably in 7th grade; she would have been in 9th. Her Sunday outfit consisted of a grey jacket & matching grey skirt, but it was those white gloves she wore that stuck out in my mind. (Remember those days, ladies?) I wondered who she was as she strolled to church with her family. I thought she was cute.

Fast forward three years. Yours truly got active as a high school sophomore, joining both the yearbook staff & Choraleers. Nancy was in both, unbeknownst to me. Not sure just who introduced us, but we immediately liked each other. She was short (5'3" tops), but she was also very attractive. Deep down I loathed the fact that she was literally engaged to a student teacher she had met at NCHS the year before.

'However, we got along as friends. She always said "hi" with a wink whenever you passed her in the hallways. (She reserved that solely for people she genuinely liked.) We used to talk about comedians on TV that we liked, such as Jack Benny & Bob Hope. We were both fans of the "Garry Moore Show", on which a young Carol Burnett served as third banana.

Moore put a lot into his variety show. One of the weekly highlights of it was a segment where Garry, clad in overcoat & fedora, would walk up to a street lamp post on stage & describe events from a long ago year.

Nancy & I had watched one particular show the night before. We may have been in study hall together, but we simultaneously chimed in unison to what Garry had said on that segment: "Yes, it was that wonderful year ~~~ 1929!" We both broke up laughing.

What Nancy taught me was how to be friends with a really pretty girl. Let's face it, teenage boys have raging hormones. No need to lust after her, although that summer of '61 she did look gorgeous in those tiger striped shorts when I ran into her in the center of town! Her white blouse added to the allure.

Nancy did marry that teacher. She was young when she did so & it didn't work out. I sensed sparks flying between those two when I saw them in town a few years later ~~~ and not of the positive kind. But I was immersed in studies at the American Academy of Dramatic Arts at the time & was flirting like crazy there.

———————————

Fast forward to 2011.

I was busy trying to update the 1963 NCHS class roster in preparation for our 50th reunion. I contacted Bailey Stewart of NCHS '61 so I could get ahold of the older siblings of some missing classmates of mine. Spotted Nancy on the 1961 reunion website & I sent her an e-mail via that site. I was hoping she'd remember me, but I didn't get my hopes up. Then ~~~ voila! ~~~ she promptly wrote back & we picked up where we left off as friends!

She & my wife Nan became fast friends as well! Nancy invited us to her 50rh reunion, which was going to be held very soon at that point. She said she had taken dancing lessons so she could "dance, dance, dance" at her reunion. (Amazingly she'd never learned to dance!) Unfortunately I was still working then & we couldn't get away for it.

But we invited Nancy to a four-day NCHS "mini-reunion", which we held here in North Charleston in late March of 2012. At that "mini" I pulled her aside at Andolini's & told her privately how I had a "crush" on her back at NCHS. Her pretty eyes widened & lit up in that "Nancy sparkle" of hers. She knew I was married then, but she really loved my compliment. (She had retired by then, having been an executive with Wells Fargo.) Though successful in big business, Nancy was unlucky when it came to love. She told Nan & I that her second husband ran off with his secretary was Nancy was unable to conceive. She never had children.

I was out by our mailbox by the road checking that day's deliveries when Nancy came strolling over to our place from her nearby hotel. She caught me off guard when she suddenly came up & embraced me, giving me a very warm kiss on the lips. After we broke the hug, she she said, "I shouldn't have done that", to which I replied: "That's okay. I didn't mind". (In reality she had just fulfilled a teenage fantasy of mine.)

Nancy went out to lunch with Nan & I after that. She could be stubborn, as she was adamant about paying for us. She did this a couple of times when we went out to dine.

Beneath that cosmopolitan sophistication she projected at that time was a sharp, but subtle sense of humor. It was like Nancy & I clicking on old gears again. For instance, I asked her why she was overindulging in so many community activities since her retirement. She replied by telling me: "I have trouble saying "NNNNNNN ~~~ Yes!"

She was living in San Francisco then. I chided her about walking the hills of that city in high heels. She said she was used to it. But I thought that would be tough on her feet, as she lived on Lombard Street.

Nancy was very much involved with the San Francisco Symphony. She thought maestro Michael Tilson Thomas was a musical genius & that she'd like to date him, after which she chuckled in that way of hers & said: "It's too bad he's gay!"

Nan & I invited Nancy to the 50th reunion of NCHS '63. She was really looking forward to it, as she was to subsequent visits to Charleston. (Nan even said she'd allow me to have a slow dance at the reunion with Nancy, as she knew how I felt about her.)

We drove Nancy back to her hotel after dinner the night before she left. She hugged us &, afterward (in that Nancy manner of hers), kissed two of the fingertips on her left hand & placed them on our respective right necks. The three of us were very much looking forward to more visits with each other.

Then, at the beginning of July, Nancy phoned us long distance. Nan answered the call. Nancy told her that she was dying. She had just returned from her doctors & had received the terrifying news that she had a terminal form of rapidly advancing cancer.

Nancy Blair passed away in San Francisco at age 69 in mid-August.

Nan was really devastated at all this happening. I was the one who had to be strong for my wife. (Thank You, Lord, for guiding us through it.)

We did communicate with Nancy for awhile by both phone & e-mail (primarily the former). I told her that someday she & I would have that promised dance. I even told her the name of the song I'd picked out for that occasion. (Maybe we'll have that dance in Heaven.)

The song I selected for our dance was composed by Henry Mancini. Listening to it I get the impression of a lone couple on the dance floor in the wee small hours of the morning doing a nice slow dance to it.

Mancini recorded the best version of it. Give a listen to it on Youtube sometime & you'll hear what I mean.

The song is called "Dreamsville".

L to R: Mary (Riggio) Tiani, Fran Ireland, & Nancy
(in white) at March 2012 "mini-reunion"

VROOOM!!!

(Reeves Callaway)

This author admits he's mechanically inept. My late wife Nan, on the other hand, was not.

"What are you going to do when I'm gone?", she used to say of my mechanical shortcomings.

"Call somebody who knows what they're doing!", I replied.

But Reeves Callaway certainly is not like me in that regard. As a youth in Connecticut he used to take apart the family lawn mower and then try to put the engine on his bicycle. He always wanted to know what makes things work ~~~ & still does. He did not inherit such skill from his father, but rather from his mother. (His dad was apparently like me in that regard.)

A 1966 graduate of New Canaan High School, Reeves earned a BA in Fine Arts at Amherst College. But his first love was (and is) the automobile.

He was given a 1955 Ford Thunderbird for his 16th birthday. On its first drive he drove it over to a friend's house. The friend's little sister took the "T'Bird" out of park & it rolled down an incline, crashing rear end first into an oak tree. Thankfully the little girl was unharmed, but the car was out of action for the next 6 months.

Reeves has become a very successful businessman as a result of all the abovementioned. But he began all this by becoming a racecar driver. His initial race car was a Deserter GS, made by the Dearborn Automobile Co. He began thinking: "How can I build automobiles like this very clever execution from Marblehead Massachusetts."

He worked at Autodynamics in Marblehead, MA, And became their lead fabricator, truck driver, and factory race car driver. He won the national championship in 1973, and shortly afterwards ran out of money. He gave up the dream of being world champion and began producing turbocharger kits in the back of his garage in Old Lyme Connecticut He began in 1976 to build turbocharged kits for BMW's. He did likewise for Volkswagen & Mercedes, among other European automakers. (Reeves would have undoubtedly loved the "souped up" police cars that were, in reality, VW "Beetles", over in Munich when I was there in the late 1960's.)

In building his turbocharged engines for these cars he had the foresight to make them emission compliant. This was the start of Callaway Cars. This company today is the specialist partner for General Motors and produces automobiles like the Corvette, Camaro, Silverado, Tahoe, Cadillac that are available as new cars through General Motors dealers using the Callaway name plate similar to Mercedes use of AMG for its high-performance models. You can walk into a Chevrolet Callaway dealer today, and drive out with a 560 hp suburban!

Right at the start he hired Paul Deutschman, the remarkable designer & engineer from Montreal who has had so much to do with the success of Callaway Cars. When one thinks of Callaway Cars today in this country, one thinks of the Chevy Corvette. Callaway Cars has supercharged the engines so a Callaway can go 206 MPH & still get over 29 miles to the gallon.

"GM has done all the heavy lifting of cost control," Reeves said, "and the magnificent engineering, and imagine, we get to use that car as our starting point. These assets are rarely available to the specialist constructor."

Callaway Cars is based in Old Lyme Connecticut and has operations in both Southern California & Heilbronn Germany.

NEXT STOP: MADISON AVENUE

(William Esty)

Let's run it up the flagpole & see who salutes it!

Let's put it on the subway & see if it goes out to Flatbush!

Advertising aficionados are certainly familiar with the name William Cole Esty (1895-1954). He was an ad executive who founded his own company in 1932 after a seven year stint at J. Walter Thompson, naming the company after himself. He was married to actress/singer/arts patron Alice Swanson (1904-2000).

William Esty & Co. scored big early on, landing the R.J. Reynolds Tobacco Company, makers of Camel cigarettes & Prince Albert tobacco. The Esty agency landed other R.J. Reynolds brands such as Cavalier, Winston, Salem, Doral, & other cigarettes as the years went on. "More doctors smoke Camels than any other ciga-rette", read one ad copy created by Esty & Co. They also created: "Winston tastes good like a cigarette should".

Landing the Colgate-Palmolive-Peet Company's soap accounts helped place Esty & Co. in the top 10 advertising agen-cies. They were a prominent part in the advertising done on TV in its infancy.

Esty & Co. continued expanding their accounts with O-Cel-O Sponges & General Mills. But they also had their setbacks as well, especially when Colgate moved their business over to the Ted Bates Agency a year after founder Esty's passing. (They eventually got it back in 1964; such is life on Madison Avenue.)

William Esty & Co. merged with the Ted Bates Agency in 1982. This was (at the time) the biggest merger of two advertising agencies. Bates, in turn, merged with Saatchi & Saatchi four years later.

WALL STREET: QUO VADIS?

(Alfred Hayes)

I remember when I was a college Student at Buffalo State College many years ago. I decided to take a couple of electives during time frames that lasted but 3 weeks during the summer. One of them was either Macro or Micro Economics (I honestly forget which). Speaking of forgetting, it was very easy to forget what all had been crammed into me once that course was over.

Not so for a person such as Alfred Hayes, however.

Alfred was a prominent American banker that was considered to be an expert when it came to international finance. He had a reputation for being as quick as lightning when it came to math.

He was born on the 4th of July in 1910 in Ithaca, NY. His father taught constitutional law at Cornell. Alfred graduated from Yale in 1930, then spent a year at the Harvard Graduate School of Business Administration, whereupon he was given a Rhodes Scholarship to Oxford. He joined the City Bank Farmers Trust Company (now Citibank) as an investment analyst in 1933. He switched to the bond department of the National City Bank in 1940. He moved to the investment department of New York Trust two years later.

Following service as an officer in the U.S. Navy during World War II, Alfred continued his upward climb. This led to his becoming vice president of New York Trust's foreign division in 1949.

With his solid background in economics, Alfred was a logical choice to succeed the embattled Allan Sproul as Chairman of the Federal Reserve Board in 1956. He was very much a conservative money manager that did battle with inflation.

Though he came to the aid of Great Britain by persuading some bankers to prop up their monetary system with a multibillion dollar credit deal in the mid-1960's, he supported President Gerald Ford when he refused to bail out New York City from its financial woes during the 1970's. (Remember that front page headline on the front page of the New York "Daily News" back then, gang? It read: "Ford to City: Drop Dead".)

Alfred decided to leave the Federal Reserve Chairmanship in 1975, He was succeeded by Paul Volcker. He closed out his distinguished banking career by serving as chairman of Morgan Stanley International until 1981.

Alfred Hayes passed way in New Canaan in October, 1989, at age 79.

THE HUBBLE? MAN, THAT'S FAR OUT!

(Richard Scott Perkin)

To those not familiar with the world of big business, the name Perkin-Elmer may sound cartoonish. I assure you its not.

Dick Perkin had been working for a Wall Street brokerage outfit when he first met Charles Elmer. The latter had been giving a lecture & the two got talking to one another afterward. Both had a mutual interest in astronomy, so in 1937 they decided to go into business for themselves. Initially it was an optical design & consulting company. During World War II their firm got into the analytical-instruments business.

Dick was the first president of Perkin-Elmer, which was headquartered in Norwalk, CT. He became chairman of the board in 1960. The company is officially listed as an electronics firm.

Perkin-Elmer got into competition with IBM in the early days of computer manufacturing. The company merged with another S & P 500 firm, EG & G, in 1999, but have retained the name of Perkin-Elmer. The company has bought many labs & such since then, which brings to mind this old routine from comedians Marty Allen & Steve Rossi. The latter is interviewing an African tribal chieftan (portrayed by Allen) in a remote part of that continent:

> ROSSI: Tell me, what is the law of the jungle?
>
> ALLEN: The big animals eat the little animals.
>
> ROSSI: We call that survival of the fittest.
>
> ALLEN: We call it free enterprise.

Not everything has come up roses for Perkin-Elmer. They were commissioned by NASA to construct the optical components of the Hubble Space Telescope in 1979. It took them two years to build it, but it was fraught with problems. Miscalibration allegedly caused a spherical aberration, which was discovered once the Hubble got into orbit. Perkin-Elmer allegedly knew of this problem prior to the launch, but apparently never informed NASA about it. Thus a separate repair mission was sent up to fix the huge telescope.

NASA sued Perkin-Elmer & was subsequently awarded 15 million dollars.

But both founders were long gone by then. Dick Perkin passed away in 1969 at age 63 while on a business trip.

NASA apparently didn't hold the two founders responsible, as they named two craters on our moon after the two founders of Perkin-Elmer.

THE COMBATIVE BUSINESSMAN

(Rawleigh Warner, Jr.)

Many years ago my maternal grandparents took my mother to a Vaudeville show. My mom said it was awful, telling me the only performer that was any good was a young dancer named Ray Bolger. She also told me of one allegedly comic routine:

One guy, clad in pajamas & a nightcap, entered from stage right carrying an oil can in his hand. The other fellow on stage left asked him: "Why are you carrying that oil can to your bedroom?", to which the guy on stage right replied: "Because I've got to get up oily in the morning!"

(Obligatory drum roll with rim shot.)

And then folks wondered why Vaudeville died.

Well, in the case of business executive Rawleigh Warner Jr he was not noted for such humor.

Rawleigh was born in Chicago in 1921 & was raised in the northern suburbs of that city. He, like his father, went to Princeton. Following his graduation from there in 1943 he served in a U.S. Army artillery outfit in Italy during World War II. There he was awarded both a Silver & Bronze Star, as well as a Purple Heart.

After the war, just like his dad, he became an oil executive. He joined Socony Mobil & began his climb up the corporate ladder. He became president of that company in 1965. A year later the firm changed its name to just Mobil. Rawleigh also did away with the longtime Pegasus logo of that company & gave their various gas stations much needed face-lifts.

As chairman he expanded oil exploration from Canada's North Atlantic to the Gulf of Mexico, as well as Europe's North Sea. With OPEC gaining strength he appointed a Saudi to the board of Mobil.

But the gas crisis of the 1970's caused the public to turn against the oil companies & the escalating prices. Here Rawleigh became combative, having his PR people place op-ed articles in major U.S. newspapers, spelling out Mobil's position through all this. He also put forth attempts at good will, as Mobil sponsored PBS' "Masterpiece Theater". But overall, with his own toughness, he tried to create a swaggering identity for Mobil.

Not all was success under Rawleigh. Mobil's purchase of Montgomery Ward turned into a financial fiasco. Attempts at hostile takeovers of both Conoco & Marathon Oil also failed, although Mobil was able to acquire smaller oil companies.

Rawleigh Warner Jr stepped down as Mobil's chairman in 1986. He passed away in 2013 at age 92.

ACHTUNG, HERR FRAULEIN!

(Northam Warren)

You ladies owe a debt of gratitude toward Northam Warren. He created the Cutex Cuticle Remover, among other things.

Northam was born in 1878 & hailed from Kansas, studying chemistry at the University of Kansas. He went to work for Parke, Davis, & Company in Chicago after graduation. He eventually transferred through that company to New York City in 1907.

But he wanted to branch out on his own &, with financial assistance from his new bride, began his own business as a drug broker in 1910. He was in a one room office on West Broadway when he started this enterprise. A year later he created the formula for the Cutex Cuticle Remover. With that success under his belt he formed the Northam Warren Corporation in 1915.

It was soon after that when Cutex introduced nail tints, followed three years later by liquid nail polish. By 1928 Cutex pretty much cornered the market, at least for a while, with the introduction of an acetone-based nail polish remover. Cutex became the largest nail care brand in the United States for the rest of the 20th century.

Northam's company moved from New York City to Stamford, CT, in 1939. By the time of Cutex's purchase by Chesebrough-Ponds in 1960, Northam's products were sold in 109 countries, Revlon now owns the Cutex brand, which it has since 2016.

Northam Warren passed away in 1962 just one day before his 84th birthday.

SHE WAS DEFINITELY AHEAD OF HER TIME

(Dr. Emily Barringer)

You may not be familiar with that name, but Dr. Emily Dunning Barringer was a true pioneer in her field. Her story is rather remarkable.

Emily was the older sister of Dr. Henry Sage Dunning, whom you'll read about shortly in this section. She was born in 1876 in Scarsdale, NY, to a wealthy family. Unfortunately, that family fell on hard times & things got so bad that a friend of her family suggested that Emily should become a milliner's apprentice. Her mother didn't like that idea at all, insisting that her daughter go to college. A family friend, Dr. Mary Corinna Putnam Jacobi, recommended the medical preparatory course at Cornell University. Emily's uncle, Henry W. Sage, was a founder of Cornell & he agreed to pay her tuition. Other relatives chipped in to help defray Emily's expenses.

After graduating in 1897, Emily attended the College of Medicine of the New York Infirmary. That school would merge with Cornell during her sophomore year & she earned her medical degree from it in 1901.

Despite her high grades, Gouverneur Hospital in New York City rejected her application for an internship there. Undaunted, Emily enlisted the assistance of various political & religious figures locally. This time Gouverneur relented & Emily became the first woman ever to be accepted for post-graduate surgical training in service to a hospital.

However she had a very rough time there from the other medical residents. They gave her difficult ward duties & "on call" schedules. She wrote about all this harassment in her autobiography, "Bowery to Bellevue: The Story of New York's First Woman Ambulance surgeon". She was a woman doctor on New York's Lower East Side & her complaints about the treatment she received was picked up by the local city newspapers, who ran feature stories about her.

Emily did marry a fellow physician, Dr. Benjamin Barringer, m in 1904, just after she completed her residency. Their union produced a son (Ben) & a daughter (Verona).

She served as vice chair of the American Women's Hospitals War Service during World War I. There she led a campaign to get ambulances over to the fighting in France.

Emily was very much an advocate of women's suffrage. She joined the gynecological staff of New York Polyclinic Hospital & also was attending surgeon at the New York Infirmary for Women & Children, where she specialized in the study of venereal disease. She did likewise for the Kingston Avenue Hospital in Brooklyn.

During World War II she helped organize the American Women's Hospital in Europe. This provided medical & surgical care both during & after the war. Emily's influence also helped pass the Sparkman Act, which gave women permission to become commissioned officers.

There was a 1952 motion picture, "The Girl in White", based on Emily's life. The role of Emily was portrayed by June Allyson.

Dr. Emily Dunning Barringer resided in both Darien & New Canaan for many years. She passed away in New Canaan in 1961 at age 84.

Barringer at her 1901 graduation

Emily Dunning Barringer as a resident at Gouverneur Hospital in New York City

REPRESENTING NEW CANAAN IN HARTFORD

(Richard Brinckerhoff)

Diversity was the name of the game for Dick Brinckerhoff during his time here on earth.

Born in Stamford in 1919, he graduated from Williams College in 1941. He wasn't sure right after graduation what career he would pursue. But things were happening elsewhere in the world that soon affected him.

World War II was on, although the United States had yet to enter the fray. Dick had heard that Pan American Airways was shipping planes & other military materiel over to North Africa to quietly aid the British & other allied countries in their fight against Nazi Germany there. He was in Accra in the Gold Coast (now Ghana) delivering military materiel when the Japanese bombed Pearl Harbor.

Given a choice between returning to the U.S. to await the draft or be given a commission in the Army Air Corps, Dick chose the latter, becoming a second lieutenant. He continued shipping supplies to North Africa & eventually did likewise for the China-Burma-India sphere of operations. He was awarded the Bronze Star & ended up his military service as a major.

But Dick had other military duties to perform late in the war. He helped plan logistics for the Yalta Conference in February, 1945. Dick & a colleague were to deliver a secret message from FDR to Winston Churchill. The duo got to meet Sir Winston & enjoyed a five minute conversation with him.

Like many others, Dick was not alone in saying that World War II was the most exciting period of his life.

After the war he became a partner in his father's Stamford law firm. He & his wife Catherine moved to White Oak Shade Road in the early 1950's. He soon became a very active member of the community.

He was active on the town council, serving on several boards & commissions, especially those concerned with the use of land. He was on the building committees for both the new West School & the YMCA. Though a Republican, Dick was appointed a judge in the New Canaan courts by Democratic Governor Abraham Ribicoff. He was eventually elected to the Connecticut State Assembly in 1970, serving there for 10 years. He often didn't adhere to the Republican party line while he was in Hartford. For instance, he successfully worked to bring low-cost housing into New Canaan.

Dick was very active in St. Mark's Episcopal Church for many years & also volunteered years later at the new Waveny Care Center.

Richard Brinckerhoff did a lot of living during his 85 years on earth. He passed away in Norwalk Hospital on December 30, 2004, at age 85.

THE THINKING PERSON'S PASTOR

(Rev. Loring D. Chase)

"And they went with haste, and found Mary and Joseph, and the babe lying in a manger."
— Luke 2:16

It is on that same aforementioned LP record, "A New Canaan Christmas Eve", that Rev. Chase read from the Gospel according to Luke. It seemed quite apropo that a little baby in one of the pews in the sanctuary began crying as he read that verse.

Rev. Chase preferred being called "Chuck" by the adults in the congregation. He had the pastorate there from 1950 through 1963. His sermons had a way of drawing people in.

"I want you to think of me as not standing here in the pulpit, but as walking down the aisle", he began a sermon in January of 1956. "I'm half-way to the back of the room. Now I'm in the narthex. I've opened the door to the outside. You can hear the traffic. You can feel the draught of air rush in.

"How do you feel about this open door? Does it make you suddenly restless, eager to get outside these four walls? Does it make you suddenly fearful that someone uninvited may walk into the room & make a scene? Are you afraid that a thief may slip through & into the coatroom? Do you shiver because the incoming air is cold? Or do you begin to daydream, your mind set off by the movement outside? Does your mind leap ahead to the places you plan to go? Or have you mentally taken off for home already? If so, come back! I promise not to talk beyond the scheduled time."

(My many thanks to William Gardner for allowing me to quote from his book, "Canaan Parish: 1733-2008", the two paragraphs above.)

Rev. Chase was born in Greenfield, MA, in 1916. His father was also a Congregational minister.

He attended Middlebury College before earning a Bachelor of Divinity degree from the Yale Divinity School in 1941. He married Helene Cosenza in 1940 & they had a pair of sons, Chris & Dave.

"Chuck" Chase was formally ordained as a minister at the Congregational Church in Ledyard, CT, in 1941. In those days Ledyard was quite the rural area. After serving as a Minister-at-Large in the rural Congregational Churches from 1944 to 1947, he accepted a calling to become the first ever associate pastor at the Congregational Church of New Canaan. The Rev. Merrill Fowler Clarke was nearing retirement age & was most impressed with his associate. Rev. Clarke sensed how the community was changing in 1950 when he actually retired & he thought young "Chuck" would be a wise choice for a growing congregation. The congregation agreed.

New Canaan only had about 8,000 residents in 1950. It grew by at least 5,000 more by the time I graduated NCHS in 1963. Growth of the town meant expansion of the church building during the mid-1950's, as additional classrooms, a parlor, & a children's chapel were added. A new Aolean Skinner Pipe Organ was donated to the church by the late Thomas J. Watson in 1957.

Speaking personally, I enjoyed the Congregational Church. Though some of my classmates thought Rev. Chase to be aloof, I didn't find him that way. But his demeanor seemed to command respect.

I was certainly active in the church, especially as a teenager. I well remember the dinners we used have on late Thursday afternoon prior to choir rehearsal. Usually they were just generic chicken & turkey pot pies purchased at the A & P on nearby Pine Street. But it was a great time of fellowship in the lecture room. Ditto Pilgrim Fellowship, which usually met on late Sunday afternoons/early evenings. Have a good many autographs from friends in my quartet of NCHS yearbooks which mention "What a blast we had in PF!".

I probably got to virtually every part of the church building, including the rafters from the 1841 construction. It was definitely built to last!

But I'm getting carried away here.

Rev. Chase accepted a calling to Westmoreland Congregational Church near our nation's capital early in 1964. Frankly, I missed his presence in New Canaan, as did many others. He was, in my opinion, a man who "walked the walk".

Rev. Loring DuBois Chase & wife Helene retired to Keene, NH, where he passed away at age 87 in 2004. His earthly remains are interred in Marlborough, NH.

Eldest son Chris Chase said this of his father when he eulogized him:

"My father had the rarest of gifts: he knew *exactly* who he was....He was, in fact, an earnest man.

"(T)he word earnest is easily misunderstood. *Anxious* people fear the future; *zealous* people try to master it; the earnest stay the course of the present, fraught with ambiguity as it may be, open to such possibilities as they emerge. To be earnest is not to find the silver lining in the cloud; it is to catch the rideable wave that suddenly & unexpectedly appears in the midst of an ocean storm."

Rev. Chase never had any dramatic training, yet he possessed a fine speaking voice. I can still hear his voice now with this Benediction he often used:

"The Lord bless you and keep you.

The Lord make his face to shine upon you,
and be gracious unto you.
The Lord lift up his countenance
upon you, and give you peace."

– Numbers 6: 24 - 26

A TRUE LOVE OF NATURE

(Dr. Harrison S. Coombs)

If you've ever been to the New Canaan Nature Center on Oenoke, you owe a debt of gratitude to the man who envisioned it. That was the late Dr. Harrison S. Coombs.

Dr. Coombs was a doctor that, for 20 years, ran his practice out of his home on South Avenue. He served as the Senior Medical Officer for New Canaan Public Schools throughout those 20 years. He was not only on the Board of Genesis, Inc., but was one of its founders. This was a community self-help drug treatment center.

Though he was a children's doctor, he was devoted to nature as well. He was very active in the Audubon Society back in the days of the old Bird Sanctuary on Old Stamford Road. But he dreamed of starting a nature center that would be larger & more diverse than the Bird Sanctuary.

He sought the aid of Susan Dwight Bliss & Marion Dickerman in fulfilling his vision. Many others from town came on board as well. Ms Bliss set aside the back 40 acres of her property, including the outbuildings. Dr. Coombs' dream became a reality. He spent many hours poring over blueprints so classrooms could be established on Ms Bliss' former property. Classes included not only bird & insect study, but trees & flowers, reptiles & amphibians, & also both fresh & salt water life.

It was only natural that Dr. Coombs became the initial President of the New Canaan Nature Center Association. By 1969 the Nature Center was indeed a reality. His oldest daughter, Lee

(Coombs) Benjamin, said that "(h)is vision shaped the start of a wonderful town jewel.

Classes & various activities continue today for everyone from pre-schoolers to seniors. There are both in-school & after-school programs & presentations held there. These continue during the summer months. A professional director-naturalist is employed there. There's also an active horticulture & botany program in the Nature Center's greenhouse.

Sadly, Dr. Harrison S. Coombs did not live long enough to truly enjoy the fruits of his dedication to the Nature Center. He passed away at the young age of 50 in 1971 while playing tennis with his wife Libby at the New Canaan Field Club. But he certainly left a most lasting legacy.

A MARRIAGE MADE IN "THE NEXT STATION TO HEAVEN"

(Peter & Ingrid Deane)

Peter Deane & Ingrid Girard were high school sweethearts at NCHS. True, he was in the class of 1959 & she in the class of 1962, but they definitely clicked as an "item"!

Let's talk about Peter first.

Pete & his family moved to New Canaan from Darien in the mid-1940's. As time went on it was obvious that he was an exceptional athlete. He was a four-letter man in football, basketball, baseball, & track. For many years he held the record for the longest football run from scrimmage at NCHS. He also was on the state championship basketball team with Wilky Gilmore (see Wilky's profile under "SPORTS").

Ingrid described Pete as "a natural salesman". After graduating from Bradley University in Illinois, he went to work doing just that for St. Charles Kitchens by Girard in Pound Ridge, NY, a company owned by Ingrid's father, Raymond. Pete soon got a reputation as a top National salesman & kitchen designer. He eventually became vice president of St. Charles Kitchens. He was cited in the publication "Outstanding Young Men of America". Pete's designs were featured in such periodicals as *Better Homes and Gardens: House Beautiful; & Kitchen And Bath.*

Pete & Ingrid married in 1966. Their union produced two children, Carrie & Peter, Jr.

Pete was also a tireless worker for the New Canaan community as well. He was a member of the Jaycees & he founded Operation New Canaan, which Ingrid said, "sent monthly gift packages to local servicemen in Vietnam". He was also president of the Rotary Club. He coached Little League baseball & basketball over a seven year period. Pete also dressed himself as Santa Claus when visited children & adults in local hospitals, the Waveny Care Center, & some private homes in town.

Ingrid joined Pete in volunteering for "Christmas in April". This program came under the umbrella of AMERICARES & helped renovate & brighten homes of both indigent & elderly people. The husband & wife duo also founded the second "Safe Rides" high school group in the US, to provide rides to high school students under the influence of alcohol and/or drugs.

Peter Deane passed away quite suddenly from a massive heart attack in July, 1991, at age 51. His name has been memorialized through the NCHS Fitness Center, which was formally dedicated in June, 2014. The Dauk family of New Canaan were one of the primary benefactors of this center, which also included the generosity of other of Peter's classmates, including Dave Elders, Mike Hobbs; Carlton ("Skip") Raymond, Joe Rucci, & Walter Stewart.

So, the local football hero married the town beauty.

Ingrid began working as a professional model at age eleven in 1954. That same year her photograph won the Kiwanis Portrait contest. She continued modeling, becoming a finalist in the 1962 Miss Connecticut Pageant.

She graduated Mount Ida College in Newton, MA, in 1964, & went to work as a flight attendant (nee stewardess) for Trans World Airlines (a.k.a. TWA). As mentioned earlier, she & Pete wed in 1966. Their two children still reside in New Canaan.

Ingrid returned to modeling in 1969 by doing print ads in periodicals for Campbell Soup, Clairol, Coca-Cola, Good Housekeeping, Oil of Olay, Pan-Am, & Volkswagen. She graced the cover of such magazines covers as *Family Health, Health, & New York*.

I was sitting in my bachelor "pad" in Buffalo one night in the early 1970's when I saw an ad on TV that caused me to exclaim: "Is that who I think it is?". Sure enough, it was Ingrid. Her magazine covers had led her to be in TV commercials for such products as Advil, Brim, the aforementioned Coke, "Fortune" magazine, New York Life, Nutri-System, & the "Wall Street Journal". She primarily served as the "pitch person" in those ads & did so quite well.

In addition to the volunteer work she did with Pete, she was active with the YMCA's Tri-Hi-Y program & served on the board of the local TV station, NCTV 79.

Ingrid Deane said she retired after Pete's sudden death in 1991. Her two adult children continue operating their family's expanded business, which is now known as Deane, Inc.

Yum!

(The Deli-Bake)

Back in the autumn of 1962, when we NCHS seniors were rehearsing the trio of one-acters we referred to as "3 by 63", we feasted on products from that shop on Elm Street.

Lynn Bickley from my class used to get on our cases for eating the props. The first of those one-acters was William Saroyan's "My Heart's in the Highlands", in which I portrayed the supporting role of the immigrant grocer Mr. Kosak. His store had to have groceries & Lynn, my classmate in charge of props, supplied them. Well, as teenagers we had voracious appetites. We devoured french bread, cheese, sausages, & what-have-you from that popular shop in the center of town which Lynn had bought as props.

I'm sure my fellow classmates involved in those plays also enjoyed the fare from the Deli-Bake at any time, play or no play. The aroma of the freshly baked items enticed one to purchase them. (After all, how could anyone resist them?)

That shop at 9 Elm Street was owned by the Smith Family for many years. Prior to that it was owned by the Polzer family, who resided on Crystal Street on the left hand side of the top of the hill, in the house next to South School. (Their son Bob was NCHS '60.)

(Oh, yes: For those of you taking notes, the other two plays we presented were "The Intruder", by Maurice Maeterlinck, & "The Fatal Gazogene":, by GBS. There'll be a pop quiz afterward.)

What did others think of the Deli-Bake? Let's ask them:

Kim Keough Trinidad: "We loved their jelly donuts! I have never bought one here that even came close to the Dekli-Bake raspberry jelly rolled in powdered sugar. Wow, just saying it makes my mouth water!"

George Cody: "Warm out of the oven raisin buns!....My Aunt Rose was raised over the drug store. When my Aunt Catherine went to Maine in the summer I stayed (with Aunt Rose) to keep her company. My prime job was to go to the Deli-Bake's back door before they opened and pick up some fresh from the oven."

Linda (Baxter) Lasco: "The Deli-Bake had the BEST macaroons on the planet!"

Laura Anne Bass: "Deli-Bake made the BEST chocolate chip cookies! I loved going in there with my Mom. Sometimes I can still smell those cookies!"

Michael Ferrer: "The brownies were the best (at) the Deli-Bake!"

Patricia (Liberatore) Avallone: "While most teens went to the Elmcrest for a 15 cent English muffin & a coke, I went to the Deli-Bake where they had a huge barrel of dill pickles floating in brine. They were 15 cents also ~~~ juicy & garlicky!"

Patrick Sullivan: "Sundays after church stocking up with parents and getting hard rolls ~~~ best cold cuts, potato salad, & slaw! Then home to create our own! (Yes), great memories!"

Betty McCrteady: "Yep, Sunday after church getting cold cuts & a big submarine sandwich roll to split. My dad would doctor the sandwich with oil & spices. And my sister & I would split a big marble cookie. Delicious!"

Steve Coombs: "We always had goodies for the holidays from the Deli-Bake, with tasty fillings. I remember running in to pick up Christmas orders while my Mom circled the block because downtown was filled with Christmas shoppers."

To wrap things up, here are ***Michael Ahearn's*** memories of the Smith family:

"Harry Smith was a classic! He was a combination of WC Fields & Don Rickies rolled into one! A kind man with a great sense of humor, but very ornery towards the end of each day. Around 4 o'clock....he would retire to his office for about an hour, leaving us on our own. Son Jeff was there, but (he) was busy in the back (working) on catering orders. When (Harry) emerged we (employees) knew not to pull his tail. Methinks he liked a few "tall boys" late in the day. Jeff was a very talented chef (that created) culinary masterpieces for catering jobs. Jeff was also a master wood carver, known nationally for his talent among bird and decoy lovers.

"(I'll) never forget the aroma Sunday mornings when the hot donuts would arrive. Nothing better than downing a few hot glazed donuts before the onslaught of the post church goers.

"Very fond memories!"

So, gang, if this whetted your appetites, feel free to go grab a snack. I'll wait.

FOR WHOM WAS THIS ROAD NAMED?

(Dr. Henry Sage Dunning)

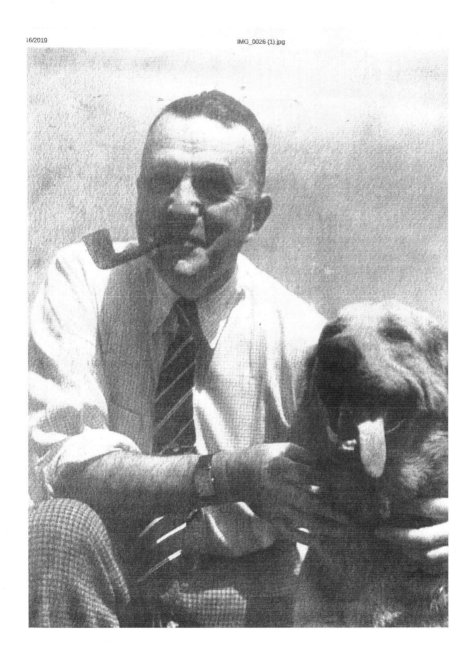

Dunning Road was named after Dr. Henry Sage Dunning.

Who was he, you might ask?

Henry co-founded the College of Dental & Oral Surgery School at Columbia University, along with his brother William. They were among a half-dozen prominent New York City dentists involved with this committee in 1916. Columbia President Nicholas Murray Butler was also closely associated with this.

Dr. Henry Sage Dunning was the head of dentistry at the old Vanderbilt Clinic on West 60th Street & 10th Avenue in Manhattan. He was one of the leading fundraisers for this new school of dentistry. Eventually this school would move to the Presbyterian Hospital on 168th Street in upper Manhattan. Henry headed the Department of Oral Surgery there for many years.

Henry served in the US military during World War I in Vichy, France. He was chief of the military facial services at the American Expeditionary Force base, smack in the thick of things at the trenches. Much like the characters of "Hawkeye" Pierce, "Trapper John", & B.J., he had little to work with in those crude makeshift field hospitals. On more than one occasion he had to put part of a face back on a comrade-in-arms that had been blown off by enemy weaponry. He developed many techniques as need be & thereby saved many lives. After he came home he collaborated on the book, "Synopsis of Traumatic Injuries to the Face & Jaws". He also performed surgeries on many cleft palates that had not been done before, as he had worked hard to develop this surgery. Oral surgery thus became his life work because of his experience in the "war to end all wars".

He was born in 1881, the son of Edwin James Dunning & Frances Gore Lang. This prominent New York family fell on hard times when Henry was a sophomore at Cornell University. He had to leave Cornell & resume his studies elsewhere. Henry earned his DMD degree at the New York City College of Dentistry in 1904 & his MD from The College of Physicians & Surgeons in 1911.

He was a long time resident of New Canaan, at first in a summer home while residing in his townhouse on 73rd Street in New York City. He did so while he still practiced his dentistry & oral surgeries. He loved both residences & would have his farm hand (New Canaan was very rural back then) milk the cows in the early morning hours & then put the milk cans on the commuter train to Grand Central., where they were picked up at the townhouse & returned empty on the evening train. Henry made New Canaan his primary residence in the early 1950's after suffering his first heart attack.

Dr. Dunning was the grandfather of two folks I befriended at NCHS back in the day ~~~ Elaine Eskesen & her late brother, Hal. Elaine said that he loved loading his adult children & young grandchildren into his "ol' broke car" & go to our nearby stream thru the hay fields & pastures to have picnics. They would drive down what was known as Pasture Lane, which in the early 1960's became Dunning Road (nicknamed "Lovers Lane" by Elaine's classmates), where they held their family picnics. She cherishes the memories of those long ago outings. Elaine would wander the property. She'd both fish in the stream & try to pan for gold (albeit unsuccessfully on the latter). It was a fantastic life, she indicated, because her granddad allowed her to be a tomboy.

Elaine also elaborated that Henry also loved to roam the fields. He would ride his horse, make simple furniture in the basement, help bale the hay, & feed his chicks in the barn. Waiting for baby laying hens to arrive was always an anticipated pleasure, as we set up lights & food for the new arrivals.

Henry also loved to hunt. Elaine said that he went to Canada many times to hunt moose, deer, & bears. There was a boar head at the top of the stairs that frightened her every time she went to her bedroom in her grandparents' house. She often wondered what her grandmother thought about that addition to the homestead.

There was one story, corroborated by her cousin Mac, where Granddad snuck out of their Weed Street home. There he found a dead squirrel on the road. So, without Grandmother's knowledge, he skinned it to both our dismay & delight. He made a small fire on the well coiver & cooked it. So delicious?

He loved smoking his pipe & walking with his dog, Lobo. Elaine said she could smell the aroma of his pipe as she trailed behind him on yet another adventure on the farm.

Dr. Henry Sage Dunning died in New Canaan in 1957.

"YOU HAVE THE RIGHT TO REMAIN SILENT. ANYTHING YOU SAY…"

(The Fairty family)

Here I am, in 2019, casually walking along Elm Street in New Canaan. Suddenly a New Canaan police officer approaches me & asks:

"Arthur Hahn?"

"Yes", I reply quizzically.

"You're under arrest!", as the handcuffs are snapped on my wrists behind my back.

"What for!!??"

"Stealing apples from Fairty's Apple Orchard."

"But I haven't done that since I was ten years old!", I protest. "I only took one or two at a time!"

"Doesn't matter. The statute of limitations on that offense is 300 years."

(With that I woke up in a cold sweat. Remind me never again to eat a peanut butter, sauerkraut, & prune pizza prior to bedtime!)

The reality is that the Fairty family is one of the oldest in New Canaan. One branch of it had an apple farm out on Old Stamford Road by Orchard Drive. Another branch of that family served with distinction at the town's Fire Department for many years. Let's talk about the latter first.

Bob Fairty was in my graduating class (1963) at NCHS. His father, Ray, was a former chief of the New Canaan volunteer Fire Department. He also served 30 years as the town's Fire Marshall.

Like father, like son, as Bob followed in his dad's footsteps. Bob served in West Germany with the US Army, but he had already joined NCFD in 1965.

Bob was initially a 1st Lieutenant Engine Captain in the NCFD. He trained probationary members. One day they used the old Valentine house on South Avenue for training purposes. The old house was deliberately filled with smoke & the men wore Scott Air Packs as they crawled around inside the house. Practice was over for quite some time when someone reported smoke emanating from that house. So, back came the entire department that was on duty to put out the fire! (The long time veterans spoke of this to the new members for years to come afterward.)

Bob became the town's first Deputy Fire Marshall in 1975, & was promoted to Fire Marshall two years later. Just like his father, he served in that latter post for 30 years. Fire inspections were part of his duties & Bob was at least partially responsible for the closing of Center School. The center of that structure was the original wood & the cost would have been very exorbitant to re-do the building. So it was closed & soon razed.

He also served as Director of Civil Preparedness (starting in 1975) & Captain of the Auxiliary Police (which he began doing in 1983). Sadly, Alzheimer's Disease afflicted Bob Fairty. He is presently in the Waveny Care Center. (He was there when we held our 50th class reunion in October, 2013.)

C.H. Fairty owned the farm on Old Stamford Road. Sadly, it's gone now, but certainly not forgotten, as the following people will attest:

Susan Swift Valdes: "(My) favorite memory of Fairty's was walking over from Summit Ridge to bring Mother fresh corn on the cob for dinner. Probably the best corn on the cob EVER!"

Karen Salley Tudor: "I grew up on Orchard Drive about 4 houses from Fairty's. I remember being given $ 1 to get 13 ears of corn for dinner...."

Robert Waibel: "I remember this, too, (as) I lived on Douglas Road. I would go on my bike for corn & get the "baker's dozen" 13 ears for a dollar....."

Donna E. Glen: "I remember running barefoot in my bathing suit with a few bucks from my mom to get a bag of corn for dinner. (This was) after spending my mornings swimming in Kiwanis Park. We later shucked the corn outside our home. Yes, my definition of summer!"

Michael Ahearn: "Got a job working for $ 2.25 an hour with my old friend Fred O'Neill. We worked nights from 6 till 9 cutting brown spots out of apples for the cider press. We'd then line the cider press frames with burlap, dump the apples in, & fold the burlap over the top. Mr. Fairty would (then) fire up the press, producing a few gallons of fresh cider. We also ate many apples....The best of times!"

Michael Ferrer: "Watched the press working that made the cider. It was the best!"

Robert Waibel: "....In the fall we enjoyed getting free samples of cider while we watched them press the apples."

Patricia (Liberatore) Avallone: "I (also) lived on Orchard Drive. In the fall my brothers & I would pick apples for 10 cents a bushel....I got poison ivy every year from doing this, but I went anyway. Great memories!!!!!"

Steve Coombs: "We lived up the hill from Fairty's on Orchard Drive. I can't ever find cider as good as theirs. We were so spoiled."

George Cody: "After every football game (we'd) stop for fresh cider. Not the hour old cider on the front porch, but the fresh & frothy cider on the pressing barn ledge."

Laura Ann Bass: "Fairty's was a staple in the fall. I remember that little shack & the apple smell. I can still see it's setting in my mind."

Deborah Bell: "(We waited) for fall to kick into full gear & headed over to watch the apple press make the cider....(Also) picking the perfect basket of apples. That first sip of that crisp apple cider puckered your mouth, but (it) was so very yummy! A very fond childhood memory!"

Karen Salley Tudor: "....The fall treat was walking over to watch the cider press & then taking some cider home. Without the preservatives we'd sometimes create 'hard cider' & it was also delicious! Great memories!"

Thanks, gang!

Bob Fairty.

"ONWARD NEW CANAAN"

(Judge Julius Groher)

Time to take a brief "R & R", gang. Ably assisting me here is Ms Lauren Wieckowski, the granddaughter of Judge Julius Groher..... And a special thanks as well to her mom, Nancy (Groher) Anderson for providing her talented daughter the opportunity to tell us about him.

"Julius Groher, known to all as 'Caesar' & 'Judge', was born in Savannah, GA, on May 2, 1915. He & his family moved to New Canaan when he was 6 years old.

"He was raised on 91 Park Street ~~~ where Bob's Sports is currently ~~~ with his two brothers & two sisters. His parents, Harry & Bessie, owned a dry goods store in town. He came up through the New Canaan school system. In high school he lettered in football, basketball, & baseball. He is also recognized for his great musical talent. While on the bus with the NCHS football team coming home after a big win over arch-rival Darien, he & the band director 'made up' a new song that was played & sung on the way home. It became 'Onward New Canaan', which is still the NCHS fight song.

"He graduated from there in 1934. He then went on to the University of Connecticut at Storrs, where he played sports & became so involved with student government that he actually became Mayor of Storrs. In a long standing rivalry between UConn & the University of Rhode Island football teams, it was tradition to steal each other's mascots before a game. When the University of Rhode Island could not find the Huskies' mascot to kidnap, they took 'Caesar' instead. As punishment they took him to the Rhode Island pep rally, but the football coach demanded they return a team member who needed to practice before the big game.

"He graduated from UConn in 1938 & was accepted at the NYU Law School. He had wanted to become a history teacher & applied to the NYU history department, but it was, at that time, more selective & harder to get into than the NYU Law School! He was asked to be on the Law Review, but unfortunately had to decline as he needed to work in order to pay for his schooling. He could be found evenings & weekends at the Elmcrest. Always an avid baseball fan, in 1938 & '39 he helped manage & coach the St. Aloysius baseball team with Father Hackett. He was also coach of the New Canaan Zebras baseball team, sponsored by his lifelong friend Izzy Cohen. He graduated from law school in 1941.

"American entry into World War II began not long after his graduation, so 'Caesar' joined the US Army. With a law degree, he imagined he would be assigned to the JAG Corps, but instead was sent to the Pacific Theater where he was a clerk for a medical unit in both India & Burma that was working to eradicate malaria. He arrived back in New Canaan in 1944 & married the love of his life, Marian Levy, on January 15, 1945.

"He started his law firm on South Avenue, practicing law with John Dolan & later with Gerald Sullivan. 'Caesar' was a practicing attorney for 50 years, as he loved his legal work so much that he never became a history teacher.

"His work made him many professional acquaintances & friends who were prominent in New Canaan, such as Sloan Wilson, the author of 'The Man in the Grey Flannel Suit' (see WRITERS).

He was instrumental in acquiring the Lapham estate for the town & for bringing in Joe Sikorski to coach football at NCHS. He was also the local attorney for David Kearns, who was president of Xerox. In an amusing story still told by 'Caesar's' children, Mr. Kearns had the honor of meeting the Pope in Vatican City. When he got there he was met by an American priest who was there to chaperone him during his visit. When he asked Kearns where he lived, he replied New Canaan. Immediately the priest lit up & said that was where he grew up. The priest then said: 'Oh then, you must know Judge Groher". Mr. Kearns replied of course. Later he told 'Caesar' how he was floored that at the Vatican of all places he met someone who knew his lawyer. It's a real testament to 'Caesar's' character & profession that everyone knew Judge Groher.

"He loved New Canaan & was heavily involved in many aspects of town government, including the Register of Voters; served on the salary committee for public schools; often chaired town meetings; was chairman of the zoning board of appeals; was third town Selectman (twice); & Senior Judge of Town Court.

"He could usually be found prior to work at the Deli-Bake, having coffee & a muffin with the 'Breakfast Club', which consisted of Ed Janis, Reggie Reynolds, & Pete Raymond, to name a few. After work he held 'court' at Pierre's (a.k.a. Izzy's Place), Fat Tuesdays', or the Gates, depending on the decade.

"He raised his family ~~~ Mark (born 1948), Elizabeth ("Betsy") (1951-2018), Nancy (born 1953), & Robert ("Bob") (born 1956) ~~~ at 23 Douglas Road & eventually at 18 Tommy's Lane. (Home of the Tommy's Lane Tigers!!!!)

"In later years when New England winters became too much to bear, he & Marian began splitting their time between New Canaan

& Laguna Woods, CA. When he retired at age 80, they moved to California full time to be near their daughters & grandchildren. He was never happier when he was surrounded by his grandchildren (Luisa, Hart, Anyel, Alexandra, Zack, Colin, & Lauren), who all loved his stories of his time in India & his old football days, as well as hearing his vast knowledge of both American history & baseball.

"Judge Julius Groher died surrounded by family on March 16, 2004. You can visit him at his bench on the corner of South Avenue & Farm Road, near his old home on Tommy's Lane."

Thanks, Lauren. Ya done good!

"POINTSET-TAH OR POINTSETT-E-AH?"

(Stephen B. Hoyt)

If you invented a time machine to take you back to, say, 1959 New Canaan & you wanted to take the Cherry Street extension from Main Street eastward, well, "you can't get there from heah".

Blocking your way eastward from Main Street in 1959 would be S.B. Hoyt, Inc.. The Cherry Street extension didn't even exist.

That floral shop & greenhouse was a town fixture. The founder of that enterprise was Stephen B. Hoyt. The Hoyt family are long-time New Canaanites. Stephen's granddaughter, Nancy Harding, has a love of New Canaan history much as he did.

He was a real fixture in town. Stephen served as president of the New Canaan Historical Society for two years in the early 1920's & again from 1940 till 1945. He also was a longtime member of the precursor to the Audubon Society & was instrumental in the estab-lishment of the Bird Sanctuary on Old Stamford Road. Stephen was active in the Congregational Church as well. He served as the editor of the book, "Canaan Parish: 1733-1933".

A Wesleyan graduate, Stephen B. Hoyt was born in 1887 & founded his floral business in town in 1908. He passed away in 1960 at age 73, much beloved by New Canaanites.

S.B. Hoyt & his Floral Shop.

A TIRELESS COMMUNITY WORKER

(Dorothy S. Hutchinson)

I remember that the daughter of Dorothy Hutchinson came to the 50th reunion of the NCHS class of 1963. True, she graduated two years behind us (as she was supposed to) & was there as an invited guest, as was her '65 classmate, Preston Jones (see "WRITERS").

I didn't know Nancy until then, but we became fast friends there. She told me that her mother was not in good shape, health wise, at that time. Nancy sensed the end was near.

Dorothy Swinnerton was born in May, 1922, in nearby Stamford. She, like her daughter, was a bright student. In fact, Dorothy graduated Stamford High School at age 16. Her future husband, Edwin Charles Hutchinson, came from New Haven. Their 35 year marriage produced six children. Sadly, Edwin passed away in 1977.

Dorothy began her service to New Canaan in 1968. She began that career as an executive secretary for the Special Education Office of the Public Schools. She then spent many years as Executive Secretary to the First Selectman of New Canaan. She also was an expert organizer of the annual Memorial Day Parade in town. She served New Canaan until she retired from public service at age 82 in 2004. She then got very active in the Hannah Benedict Chapter of the DAR.

She was a woman noted for her strong New England work ethic, as well as her strength of character. She was also very involved with her immediate family as well.

Dorothy S. Hutchinson passed away soon after the above-mentioned reunion, going home to be with her husband Edwin on October 22, 2013. She was a great person that very much enjoyed what she did in this life.

A PAIR OF UNSUNG CONTRIBUTORS

(Clarence & Alice King)

Chris King, Jonathan ("Jot") Ross (he of NCHS '64), & yours truly met at a '50's diner with the name of BudaBing's in Millis, MA, in May of 2018. I had needed such a trip as Nan had passed away just three months prior to that. It was a chance to catch up with some old friends with whom I went to NCHS.

Chris was only at NCHS for his & my junior year (1961-'62). Nonetheless, he's an easy guy to like & he did make many friends during his school year there. "Jot", on the other hand, I'd known since grade school when we sang in the youth choir at the Congregational Church. All three of us were members of Choraleers. (See EDUCATORS.) We "pigged out" over the HUGE breakfasts they serve at BudaBing's. Our conversation was like picking up where we'd left off more than 50 years prior to this.

Chris had New Canaan roots with his grandparents, Clarence & Alice (Seabrook) King. They are indeed worth mentioning.

Clarence & Alice resided on Silvermine Road & Mill Street at their home, which They called "Still Pond". This was where they raised their four children during the early years of the 20th century. He was an attorney that also was a professor of social work & community Organization at Columbia University. According to Chris he "rubbed shoulders with both Franklin D. Roosevelt & Al Smith", working as a "troubleshooter" for FDR's long time confidant Harry Hopkins. Clarence was very active locally with both the Red Cross & the Community Chest.

Alice was both an author & a poet. She had been a music hall singer in her youth. The King's were Quakers. After World War II they hosted a pair of "Hiroshima Maidens" that were victims of that atomic bomb blast, which virtually leveled that Japanese city. The two young women were stateside to undergo plastic surgery.

Clarence & Alice were active in both the local NAACP. As Chris also mentioned they "were active in helping people of color feel welcome in New Canaan".

Very much lovers of nature, they donated a large section of their New Canaan land to the Audobon Society. They also donated "Still Pond" to the Natural Science for Youth Foundation. This was later transferred to the New Canaan Land Trust.

Clarence & Alice King retired to Nantucket in the late 1960's, where they lived out their remaining days.

"WE JUST WANT THE FACTS"

(Chester Lewis, Jr.)

No, Chet Lewis was hardly like SGT Joe Friday on TV's "Dragnet". He was an amiable man, but he could also be very no nonsense.

Chet was born in 1925. He was a graduate of New Canaan High School & served for three years in the US Navy during World War II.

He was known as SGT Lewis when I was a kid there. He was very visible to us as teens as he taught Drivers' Ed. I had him for the classroom end of it, while another New Canaan police officer, Nick Pia, taught me how to actually drive a car. So, he taught would-be young drivers the facts (i.e., "who has the right to carry a green cane").

Chet served on the NCPD for 30 years, retiring as a lieutenant. He also founded the Lewis School of Driving in town. He was most active in the community, serving as president of both the Rotary & Exchange Clubs. He co-founded the local Pop Warner football league & was a youth advisor at the YMCA for 20 years.

Chet's first marriage didn't work out, but when he married Joann, his life began to happily turn around. With her he was able to regain his Irish identity. Joann had been born on the "Emerald Isle" & together they spent many happy days in Ireland. He even obtained his Irish citizenship before he died

Say what you will about cops sitting around eating doughnuts. Chet, contrary to the Stereotype, stayed active, as you can see above. He was a true pillar of New Canaan.

Chet Lewis passed away in February, 2006, at the age of 80.
His ashes are interred in Ireland, as are those of his mother & sister.

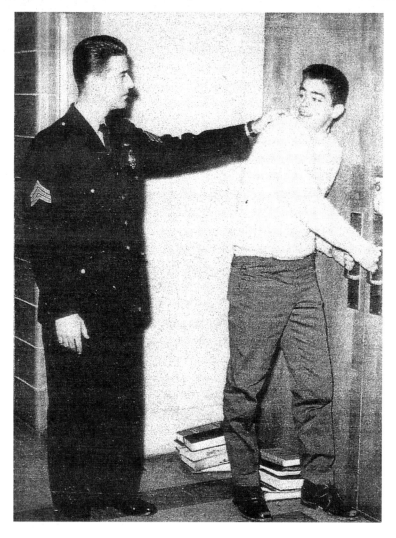

SGT Lewis putting the figurative collar on King Chapin at NCHS

"MAC"

(Charlie Maguire)

Whenever I visit New Canaan these days, I prefer going to Cherry Street East to dine.

But here we're going to be talking about another restaurant of yore. Raise your hand if you ever ate at the Elmcrest Luncheonette.

Liberace used to say on his TV show of the 1950's that "I can't go on any further without my brother, George". Well, in this instance I'm going to let my older brother, Alan Hahn, do most of this profile while I take a brief "R & R".

"As you travel uphill to the west on Elm Street, at address number 35 is the site of what used to be the Elmcrest Luncheonette. Of course, no one knew it as the Elmcrest; back then it was simply 'Mac's'. In 1954, when I worked there part-time after classes at New Canaan High, the proprietor of Mac's was Charlie Maguire. (H)e taught me a lot about the retail food business, and much more as well.

"My family had moved to New Canaan from another little town named Tonawanda, NY, in the Buffalo area....I was very pleased to see a sign in the Elmcrest window advertising a need for a part-time dishwasher. And so, after football season was over, I walked into the Elmcrest & was interviewed.

"Mr. Maguire asked me if I had done any of this sort of work before, and he showed me a US Navy Surplus Dishwashing Machine. As it happened I had used the same type of machine at a Boy Scout camp in the Buffalo area. Mr. Maguire ~~~ 'Call me Mac' ~~~ was pleased to hear this. He described the duties, hours, & pay, & I agreed to start work the next week. Mac advised me to obtain my parents' approval first, which I did & started work there early in 1954.

"I quickly learned that I could do more than just operate the dishwasher. I learned how to make ice cream sodas, milk shakes, & do a bit of cooking on a gas-fired grill in the kitchen area, as well as wait on tables & clean up at day's end.

"It was impossible not to like Mac or his wife, a former French Canadian lady whom everyone knew as 'Skeezix'. Mac & Skeezix had four daughters, two of whom worked as servers....It was very much a family affair with them & others (not related to them that once worked there.)

"Mac & his family attended St. Aloysius Church. But now for a little Maguire history.

"Prior to going into business in New Canaan, Mac had lived in Brooklyn, NY, where he operated another luncheonette....During the 1930's his luncheonette was located in the 'operating area' of a mob family, & so was forced to pay 'protection money' to a pair of toughs who stopped in weekly to pick up the payment.

"After church on Sundays Mac would take a walk in Brooklyn while Skeezix would remain home to tend to their new-born daughter.

"On one of these walks, Mac found himself in a sparsely populated area of South Brooklyn. There were very few others walking that day, except for a (lone) man about a half-block in front of him. A fairly new car drove slowly by Mac & the men inside the vehicle looked him over carefully. They suddenly shook their heads & drove up next to the other man. Suddenly there was a lot of gunfire from the car aimed at the man walking in front of him. Mac then took off very quickly for home. He told Skeezix that he he had just witnessed a gangland "hit". Needless to say they were both very worried!

"The protection money collectors returned on their usual day. But this time they asked Mac if he had seen anything on his walk the previous Sunday. He said he hadn't. They then told him that from here on he would not have to pay protection money, as long as he kept his mouth shut.

"Mac & Skeezix had thought about getting out of New York City for some time and now they thought it best to do so. Finding a newspaper listing for a vacant shop in New Canaan, they took a Sunday drive & looked over the property at 35 Elm Street. It looked like it could work & they contacted the owner to arrange a lease. They began to move their young family to New Canaan.

"By the time I made my appearance, Mac & Skeezix were well established in town. But Mac had learned a few other things in Brooklyn which helped his new enterprise.

"They contacted a dealer who could install liquid propane gas to serve his grill. He knew that ~~~ back then ~~~ electrical failures were fairly frequent in southern Connecticut. The LP gas fired grill would permit him to remain open during power outages. So it did! During the major hurricane which hit Connecticut in 1938, Mac had the only restaurant open for business for several weeks. His clientele grew rapidly.

"Mac had a great many old Navy surplus items. He had been a cook in the Navy. Some of these items included old style, heavy aluminum kettles which served as cooking pots for such (culinary items) as corned beef & cabbage on St. Patrick's Day. Not to be outdone, Skeezix used those pots to prepare French Onion Soup.

"Mac always opened the Elmcrest at 6 a.m. He made a special treat for local policemen who began their shifts then. This breakfast featured fried eggs, toast, coffee, o.j., & a ⅜" thick slab of fried ham about 5" x 9". Mac took care of the local police officers & they did the same for him.

"I remember all this warmly."

Thanks, Alan.

Yeah, Mac & Skeezix were great people!

I know that brothers Greg & David Morgan, as well as the late Ms Pat Campbell, thought likewise.

HE DID INDEED "WALK THE WALK"

(Judge Stanley P. Mead)

"This book", announced Judge Stanley P. Mead about the Holy Bible, "is your guide to life."

Judge Mead annually presented copies of the then new Revised Standard Bible to 3rd graders at the end of the Sunday school year. These Bibles were paid for by the congregation at the Congregational Church. He was always proud when he held up the Bible as he uttered the above introductory sentence.

He was a beloved figure throughout New Canaan & well respected. Several of us had him for Sunday school around 6th or 7th grade. He imparted much wisdom to us about living the life of a true Christian, putting it into perspective for our own daily living.

Judge Mead came from one of the town's oldest families. He was born in 1890 & was a 1911 graduate of Yale. He was a majority leader for 30 years in both houses of the Connecticut General Assembly. He was greatly responsible for the establishment of Connecticut's juvenile-court system. He served as a judge there for 19 years.

Again I'm going to turn this over to my older brother, Alan, for his memories of him:

"The full name of Mead Park is Mead Memorial Park, and I came to know the place as a member of the NCHS football team late in 1953. We practiced daily on a field behind what was then the high school building on South Avenue, next door to Saxe Junior High. (We) played our home games at Mead Park, which was an easy sprint from the old high school.

"After what would become an unforgettable game, our last of the fall 1953 season, we were showering in the old high school locker room & celebrating our totally unexpected 33-0 victory over Hackley Prep. (That's) when one of our coaches breathlessly announced that he had just received a phone call.... (saying) that our team had tied for the state championship in Class 'S' high schools!.... We felt special, as you might expect.

"Just a few weeks later, (however), I was asked to team with Judge Mead in a debate to be held at the Congregational Church's Pilgrim Fellowship meeting. Now as a high School senior I was more than a bit amazed to be teamed against a judge in a debate! Why me, (I wondered), and what was the debate to be about?

"Well, as the old (Bob Dylan) song went, 'The Times They Are a-Changin', for we were to discuss the status of Negro students at NCHS! As a recent arrival from the City of Tonawanda, NY ~~~ there had been **NO** Black students there ~~~ I felt seriously less than qualified for such a task, especially against a seated Judge!

"A few days later I swallowed my concerns and began what would be my very first debate. After the moderator introduced us, the Judge and I began. Judge Mead asked me what I thought of any civil rights problems at NCHS, and if there really were any such problems.

"To begin with we agreed that any uneasiness in town had eased by the recent creation of the African Methodist-Episcopal Church. (That church would eventually move to the old Methodist Church at the corner of Main & Church Streets.) But elsewhere, problems in New Jersey suburbs...where many white people felt they were being 'blacked out', (did exist).

"'So, OK', said Judge Mead to me. "Then what will we debate about?" So I hit on the recent success of the NCHS football team

"Our team ~~~ all 25 of us ~~~ included three Negro players in our ranks. Their names were Ken McCall, George Nash, and Graham Foster. (They) were excellent football players. I described how they demonstrated good sportsmanship and teamwork, ...finally concluding by noting that these three young men helped make us a winning team.....McCall would soon be elected president of his junior class. He began dating the daughter of the AME Church pastor as well. (Don't forget, several teams in major league baseball had yet to integrate, including the New York Yankees.)

"Judge Mead made it clear as the debate ended when he announced to all those assembled there that he "concurred" with (my) opinion."

Thanks again, Alan.

Judge Stanley P. Mead (who, appropriately, resided at 30 Mead Street) passed away in October, 1974, at age 84.

Have I placed him on too high a pedestal? Well, he was human. Our parents, Franklin & Louise Hahn, often sat with Alan & me in a pew or two in front of Judge Mead. When it came time to sing hymns, he could be heard in several nearby pews. He couldn't carry a tune & sang off-key. But he did indeed "Make a Joyful Noise to the Lord"!

Photo by E.J. Cyr.

"HE LOVED NEW CANAAN!"

(Carlton S. Raymond, Jr.)

So enthused his son, Greg, not too long ago when I asked if I could profile him for my book. He was all in favor of my doing it.

Everyone referred to Carlton S. Raymond, Jr., as "Pete". He was born in New Canaan in August of 1916. His father, Carlton Sr., served there as Town Clerk. Pete decided to follow in his father's footsteps when it came to civic service.

He was a star athlete at NCHS, lettering in baseball, basketball, & tennis. Two of the basketball teams he was on were state champions. Pete graduated NCHS in 1933. He went on to the American Institute of Banking, followed by the Graduate School of Banking at Brown University. He did this because he began employment at the New Canaan Savings Bank in 1935. He became that bank's president in 1973 after progressing through the ranks. It was a part of Chase Manhattan at the time of Pete's death.

He married Marjorie ("Marnee") Gage. She was the Welcome Wagon hostess for many years & founded the Newcomers Club of New Canaan, Inc. Their union produced 5 children: Carlton III (a.k.a. "Skip"), daughters Pat & Penny, & sons Greg & Bruce. Pete served in the US Army during World War II.

After the war he & Judge Julius Groher coached the New Canaan Zebras semi-pro baseball team. Pete & Julius had been teammates in sports at NCHS years before. Later on he was on the board of directors & coached both Little League & PAL baseball.

He also enjoyed his civic duty, as he served for 10 years (1953-'63) on the Commission of Public Safety, which was later split into separate fire & police committees. He was elected & served 10 years (1963-'73) as a town Selectman. He was secretary of the town's Republican committee back then. He encouraged others to do similar types of civic service, as he took great pride in his contributions to New Canaan.

Pete wore many hats. He & Police Chief Henry Keller were among local leaders who helped found the local YMCA in the late 1950's. He also served on the NCHS Athletic Board. He was on the board of directors of the local Chamber of Commerce & was a treasurer of the New Canaan Cemetery Association, which oversees Lakeview Cemetery. He served as president of the Exchange Club & was a life member of that group of civic leaders that in a Group known as the Poinsettia Club. He at one time directed the United Fund & was a governor of the New Canaan Historical Society.

But let's leave it to William Jordan who, in 1994, singled out Pete for praise, citing the fact that was responsible for the start of the success in hundreds of local homeowners & business people because of Pete's confidence in them as a banker. Mr. Jordan felt that this was the "true picture of his real service to the town".

Carlton S. Raymond, Jr., was a long time member of the United Methodist Church. He passed away in Norwalk Hospital in February of 1995.

Seated are (l to r): Judge Stanley P. Mead , CARLTON S. RAYMOND, Izzy Cohen, Riley Hogan, & Judge Julius Groher.

Standing (l to r): Charles Kelley, Dr, Thomas Cody, Bob Bliss, & unidentified gentleman.

MAN ABOUT TOWN

(John Rogers)

The John Rogers I'm profiling here was the great-grandson of famed sculptor John Rogers. (I made this disclaimer because the elder John Rogers was already profiled in the Warren Allen Smith book, "Unforgettable New Canaanites".)

This John Rogers had a sister named Laurie. She (thankfully) is still very much with us. John was born in January, 1945, and Laurie in December of that same year, in Norwalk Hospital. The two of them lived in New Canaan through the middle of 6th grade, which is when their recently divorced mother remarried & moved them to Princeton, NJ. Young John was sent to the South Kent, CT, prep school. He became Head Prefect during his senior year there. He was also awarded the drama prize for not only acting in, but designing the sets for, the school's production of "Guys and Dolls". He went on to Boston University, then to Michigan State graduate school where he received an MBA at Michigan State.

After college he returned to New Canaan with his wife, the former Judith Sanden. Initially he worked for US Plywood-Champion International, which has offices in both New York City & Stamford. Eventually he joined Paul Killiam Shows, Inc. Here he was truly in his element, as together they preserved some of the best known silent films for future generations. (See "TV & RADIO" for Paul's profile.) John worked with Paul until 1990. After that he really did become the aforementioned "Man About Town", as he volunteered his many talents to the New Canaan Historical Society, the Town Players, & the New Canaan Society for the Arts.

Their great-grandfather lived with his family on a large piece of property on Oenoke Ridge, which is where St. Mark's Episcopal Church is now located. The elder John Rogers' Studio was declared a National Historic Landmark & it was moved to the grounds of the town's Historical Society. Young John served as both curator of the Rogers Studio Museum & became a governor of the Historical Society.

He began a club called the Rogers Group, which brought together collectors of His great-grandfather's sculptures from throughout the United States. John renovated the studio, designing new lighting & building displays for the artwork.

John became president of the Historical Society, serving in that capacity from 1976 till 1980. He compiled videos of major town events, including parades, which resulted in the video, "New Canaan Celebrates". He also found time to write a book, "John Rogers and the Rogers Groups", which was published by the Historical Society. He was on the board of governors for them for the remainder of his life.

Both his business & artistic acumen were put to good use in helping to found the New Canaan Society for the Arts. He served on the board of it from its beginning. The home for it is in the old carriage barn at Waveny Park (nee the Lapham estate) & is located next to the Powerhouse there, which is home for The Town Players. Laurie remarked that the old Powerhouse was literally "John's home away from home for many years".

John's first love was the theater. He got hooked seeing Mary Martin (see "ACTORS & ACTRESSES") literally "flying" on their TV screen in the the live production of the musical, "Peter Pan". He became determined as a kid then to build a flying apparatus, which he did. He hung it from an apple tree on his parents' property. He didn't try it himself, but convinced a neighbor's young daughter to try it, which she did (without mishap, thankfully).

John was a literal dynamo with TP. He designed sets, building scale models of them & supervising their construction, doing much much of the carpentry & painting of them himself. He even managed to act in a pair of musicals that TP put on: "Guys and Dolls" & "Two by Two". He did serve as both artistic director & TP president, but he preferred doing set design above all else. One of the sets he built for either NCHS or the New Canaan Summer Theater featured a moving, steam-belching train that garnered applause from the audience!

Laurie went on to say "and then there was his love of music". He loved music of all types. He frequently made audio tapes for friends of music from various sources as gifts for both family & friends. John & his sisters visited their father in Mexico. There a singing trio gave him a guitar. He learned how to play it himself, even though he was in junior high at the time. (He did so, Laurie said, "because the girls liked it".) He did compose his own songs, which he sang around New Canaan in clubs & restaurants.

Cancer claimed John Rogers at age 51 in 1996. He was well loved by New Canaanites. Laurie said of his funeral that "St. Mark's was packed with young & old during a thunder & lightning storm that formed a perfect dramatic backdrop for the man who devoted his life to the theater".

I know Laurie, but I never knew John. I certainly would have liked to, as he & I had much in common. He seemed like quite a guy!

"SANDY"

(Phil Rose)

"Mothers of River City, heed that warning before it's too late,

watch for those telltale signs of corruption!

The minute your son leaves the house

does he re-buckle his knickerbockers below the knee?

Is there a nicotine stain on his index finger,

a dime novel hidden in the corn crib?

Is he starting to memorize jokes from 'Captain Billy's Whiz Bag'?

Are certain words creeping into his conversation,

words like 'SWELL'

and 'SO'S YOUR OLD MAN'!!!?"

The above was taken from the song "Trouble", one of the many fine numbers written by Meredith Willson (copyright 1957) for his hit musical, "The Music Man".

Phil Rose came to New Canaan in 1958 when the above mentioned show was a huge hit on Broadway. But he was the complete antithesis of "Professor" Harold Hill!

I first met him sometime in '58. He had become a member of the Congregational Church. He took a bunch of kids that were students at Saxe Junior High over to see the temporary home of the YMCA, which he had come to town to direct. I remember it was in an old house on Oenoke Ridge (which was later moved to make room for the new St. Mark's Episcopal Church). The facility didn't leave much of an impression on me. What sticks out in my mind for some strange reason were stacks of old magazines, mostly *Sports Illustrated*. (Yep, one could read about the 1955 & '56 MLB seasons in their annual "Baseball Preview" issues, which were there. They'd be worth something today.)

But Phil (whom everyone called "Sandy") was a very congenial young man. In fact, he had what some might call charisma. All of us there that day immediately came to like him.

Prior to 1956 the nearest YMCA was in Norwalk. Juvenile delinquency was on the minds of many adults back then, so a quartet of community leaders (i.e., Police Chief Henry Keller, Carlton S. Raymond Jr, Robert Brand, & Judge Stanley P, Mead) thought that New Canaan should have their own YMCA to help steer the town's youths in the right direction. (After all, they didn't want their kids to be like the ones in the song from "The Music Man"!) Roger Arthur was brought in from the Norwalk "Y" to direct operations of it in New Canaan, but not much happened until Sandy shuffled in from Buffalo.

Sandy was born in Providence, RI, in 1926. He graduated OCS at Fort Benning & became a lieutenant in the US Army. He was based in the Philippines as World War II was drawing to a close. After his 1947 discharge he received a BS in Community Organizations from Springfield (MA) College in 1951. That school specialized in physical education training, especially for those going to various YMCA's. His first assignment was starting a "Y" in Wallingford, CT. He spent 3 years there both implementing & directing it. He did much the same in Buffalo, NY.

He gained something else from Wallingford: a wife, Cynthia Clark. They eventually had 3 children ~~~ sons Eric & David & a daughter, Susan.

The "Y" had several temporary homes in town until the aforementioned Robert Brand was able to acquire seven acres of the old Hexamer-Benedict property on South Avenue just south of NCHS during the early 1960's. He was a one-man show in the early years there.

Sandy did not let the grass grow under his feet during the formative years of the "Y". Early on he organized basketball teams that played in local gyms; took the kids swimming at both the Norwalk & Westport "Y's"; began a day camp at Kiwanis Park; & started a target-shooting program on the NCPD rifle range, under the watchful eye of Patrolman Dominick Cerretani, for a good many years.

Of the Kiwanis Park day camp, Jeff Titus remarked: "My clearest memory of him was one day when I was standing next to the water's edge. I was covering my arm because it hurt. (Sandy) came up to me & asked what was wrong. He then insisted on getting me to the doctor. There they discovered that I'd fractured my wrist.... Kind of odd what we do remember."

Cheryl Poirier felt motivated by all this & more: "I spent many hours at the YMCA as a youth leader, lifeguard, swimmer, & day camp leader. His leadership & that of others at the 'Y' inspired me to go to Springfield College & seek a career in the YMCA. Although I have since changed careers, (Sandy's) influence at the 'Y' remains with me always"

New Canaan had lacked an adult education program in town, so Sandy began one at the "Y". He also founded the memorable "Teen Canteen" in the basement of Paggy's Restaurant on Main Street, opposite Town Hall. He did all this solo, but by 1960 he needed more assistance than just volunteers. So the late Richard M. Ploss was hired as program director.

As for the Canteen, Bob VanDerHeyden said that he: "helped Sandy build the Teen Canteen under Paggy's Restaurant in the late

1950's. Never had any trouble there because it was right across the street from the police station".

Nancy Harding added that "We had so much fun there on Saturday nights....It had concrete floors, but we were as happy as could be. So much for New Canaan fancy".

Melinda McKeon remembers "dancing with Sandy at the Canteen. He had a way of making each kid each kid feel special & he was a great dancer!"

Laura Anne Bass chimed in by saying "My first memories are of him presiding over the Friday night dances. (We) always had a certain distance maintained between partners....The YMCA was a very special place for me in the 1960's & early '70's. (Sandy) was the glue that held it together".

But the nomadic "Y" was running on fumes much of the time. It looked like it might even fold until the site for the new facilities was purchased on South Avenue. Soon things really began blossoming. The initial building on that site would contain New Canaan's first public swimming pool, among other amenities. Leslie Leuthold remembers "his happy twinkling eyes when we came in for the swim team".

Robert J. Waibel commented: "I remember swimming lessons from him at the 'Y'. I wasn't a very good swimmer. I'd never been able to float very well. (Sandy) would get in the pool with me & hold me up, instructing me to relax. He was patient & kind".

Dani Hutchins Mollenkamp further elaborated on his caring nature by saying: "After one of those superb swim lessons at the 'Y' he told me I should not go outside on such a cold night with wet hair. He kindly asked me to go back to the locker room & dry my hair with one of the hair dryers. Far from being annoyed, I was so very thankful he showed an interest in both my health & welfare".

A second structure on that site was built 4 years later. It would contain a gym & health rooms, as well as a wall court for handball. A third building came along sometime later, which features a second swimming pool, another health club, & a weight room, as well as a social meeting room & a student theater.

By the time of Sandy's retirement in 1983, the staff of the "Y" consisted of a general secretary, two phys ed directors, a program director, & an associate general secretary ~~~ all five of them being full-time employees. In all some 210 were on the payroll, but 200 of them were part-time. Sandy could count on 300 volunteers at the time of his retirement, but he never had a shortage of them during his 25 years as general secretary of it.

Sandy & Cynthia decided to retire to Brunswick, ME. They moved to Punta Gorda, FL, 14 years later so Phil could play more golf.

Phil Rose passed away there in 1997.

––––––––––––––––––––

To sum up Sandy here are 3 more comments:

Jill Ettinger Diamond: "I was really a shy kid, so the fact that he was approachable stood out. (I've) heard it said that 'you may not remember what a person said, but you remember how they made you feel'. In this case so true".

Karen Helle Nemiah: "Throughout my childhood he was a positive adult influence. He will forever be with me as one of the few adults who truly empathized with teens. (To both our) fears & frustrations he responded with kindness, concern, & guidance

~~~ NOT authority & mandates. He was an incredible role model".

Bruce MacDonald: "There should be a plaque for him in town. He made being a kid extra fun!"

"ONE SINGULAR SENSATION"

(The Walter Schalk Dancers)

The abovementioned Marvin Hamlisch song is probably the perfect way to sum up those that were a part of his troupes over the years.

The Walter Schalk School of Dance has been a Fairfield County fixture for over 60 years now. Countless youth learned from a master ~~~ & still do!

Walter originally hailed from Stamford. He was a young dancer who, in 1950, was a finalist at the Harvest Moon Ball held at the old Madison Square Garden on 8th Avenue & W. 50th Street. It wasn't long before he danced on the "Ed Sullivan Show". He also made televised appearances on both Fred Waring's show & Frank Sinatra specials.

Though he started out as a letterpress printer, he switched to choreography as the 1950's moved along. He was moonlighting at the time doing choreography for Broadway & summer stock musicals.

He moved to Wilton & was approached by New Canaan friends to give dance lessons for a cotillion. It wasn't long before the idea formed in his mind to teach stage dancing to local youth. Word of mouth, as any salesman knows, is the best advertisement ~~~ & the Walter Schalk School of Dance took off!

It is said he is demanding, but apparently not as much as Jerome Robbins was. Still he half-jokes that "I'm tough".

There was a 60th anniversary bash some time back in which many of his former (albeit younger) troupers donned 1940's costumes & jitterbugged away. One female former student wrote of that soiree: "Wow, I had so much fun & am still today, flying high from all the good will, fond memories, great conversations, lovely food & setting, all around fun. The only thing that hurts more than my knees & ankles is my stomach, from laughing". (This item came from the *Wilton Bulletin*.)

The response above from one Kristyn Priali typical of Schalk alumni. The ones I've known feel likewise.

Walter is very proud of both his annual Holiday Spectaculars & Spring Revues. His students get to do four or five group numbers in each production. (All the dances are done in costume, BTW.) Many of his alums have been Rockettes & others have become dancers on Broadway.

(Shortly before completing this book this author learned that the 2019 Spring Revue will be the final show produced by Schalk.)

Seven of the Schalk alum from NCHS '64 are pictured here. L to R are: Elaine Holt, Bill Blair, Bonnie Bach, Mr. Schalk, Sue Lorch, Dick Tiani, Jamsie Tiani, & Patti Liberatore.

THE EQUESTRIAN'S EQUESTRIAN

(Margaret Cabell Self)

Just about every month a quartet of local ladies gather together & dine out. All four were once members of the New Canaan Mounted Troop. I refer to their group with the title of a song from the Broadway show, "Company" (i.e., "The Ladies Who Lunch").

All four were members of the NCMT under the guidance of Margaret Cabell Self.

Margaret was usually referred to as "Nonie" by those who knew her. She founded NCMT in 1939, a part of the Junior Cavalry of America. She opened it up for both boys & girls. Coming with my family to New Canaan from the Buffalo, NY, area in the mid-1950's, I wondered what type of group this was when I first saw Suzy Thurrott decked out in her NCMT uniform. I'd been a cub scout, but had never seen anything like this before.

"Nonie" taught her pupils not only life skills, but good horsemanship as well as the grooming & care of the animals. NCMT still thrives today years after her death.

She was among the "FFV" (i.e., First Families of Virginia), Her ancestry in that state has been traced back to at least 1723. The Cabell family became very prominent through the years in Virginia politics. Though born in Cincinnati in 1902, "Nonie" was raised in Virginia. She was taught how to ride a horse before she could walk. She was known as a skilled equestrian by the time she was in her teens.

"Nonie" moved north to New York City to attend college at both the Women's School of Applied Design & the Parsons School of Design. She married Sydney Baldwin Self in 1921; he was her brother's college roommate. Together they had four children (two sons & a pair of daughters. Their youngest daughter, "Giney", has followed in her mother's footsteps when it comes to horses.

"Nonie" & Sydney moved to New Canaan in 1923. They bought horses for their farm there & she began teaching riding skills to young people in 1929. But the Great Depression hit hard & "Nonie" turned to writing books about horses & horsemanship in order to keep their horses. Among her numerous books are: "Red Clay Country"; "Horses: Their Selection, Care, & Handling"; & "The Horseman's Encyclopedia".

The Self's retired in 1962 & moved to Block Island, which is off the coast of Rhode Island. They wintered in Mexico. Sydney passed away in 1980 at age 84, with "Nonie" joining him when she passed away in 1996 at age 94.

Margaret Cabell Self is on the right as she & Deborah Hicks
are about to fly to Ireland in December, 1958.

SHE ANSWERED HER CALLING

(Sister Rita)

Yes, she did have a calling. So, too, did movie actress Dolores Hart a generation later, for she also became a nun.

Sister Rita came to St. Aloysius Church here in 1947. She resided in a convent then, which was located in the old Lockwood home on Cherry Street. She was a part of the Sisters of Notre Dame de Namur, which was in Westport. She & her fellow sisters helped plan a parochial school for the St. Aloysius Parish.

The path to that parochial school was a long one. In order to give Catholic children religious education back then they had to dispatch a school bus to the then new South School, where Father Edmund Hussey would gather his youthful flock back to the church. (Kids at Center School were luckier; all they had to do was walk across the street!)

It was elderly Father William J. Fox who had long envisioned this parochial school. He announced in April, 1954, that it was going to finally be built. Parishner William H. Orpet was Selected as chairman of the fund drive for it. (Father Fox was appointed a Monsignor in July of that year by Pope Pius XII.)

In the meantime Sister Rita left a lasting impression with the youth of St. Aloysius. She was the director of the church's children's choir. She also taught Gregorian Chants via rote and gave piano lessons & encouragement to young musicians. She also helped prepare these youth for First Holy Communion.

St. Aloysius Parochial School formally opened for business in October, 1956. Initially it was occupied by 6th graders from New

Canaan Public Schools. New Canaan was growing steadily in population then & a new high school was under construction at South Avenue & Farm Road, which wouldn't formally open until midway through the 1956-'57 school year. It was decided to make the 6th grade a part of Saxe Junior High, but they had to be taught in two area churches (St. Aloysius & the First Congregational) until the new high school was completed.

Sister Rita taught third grade when the parochial school opened. She was also the music teacher there as well.

But her time there was brief, as she was transferred to parishes in both Westport & Providence before returning to St. Aloysius in 1963 after a five year absence. She stayed at St. Aloysius from then until her retirement in November, 1990. She was both well loved & respected by the students there.

Each doughnut gets Sister Rita's personal attention

WHATEVER BECAME OF FINAST AND THE A & P?

(Walter Stewart's Market)

Finast used to be on Main Street opposite East Avenue. The A & P was on Pine Street. (Pay attention to that, gang. I'll have a pop quiz later.)

But Walter Stewart's Market has certainly survived them! The Stewart family has always been one that gives back to the community in charitable endeavors.

Founded in 1907 on Main Street opposite Town Hall by the first Walter Stewart, it was a cash-&-carry operation. True, they did deliveries back then ~~~ via horse & wagon. This was later upgraded to Model T Fords doing same.

Young Walter took the reins in 1933 & guided them in their relocation to Elm Street west of Park Street & opposite the train station. The unique concrete & glass design was done by architect Victor Christ-Janer. It has been expanded through the years.

Present day owner Bailey Stewart opened a liquor store on the premises in 1974. He now has his nephews, Alex & Doug, run the store operations.

Yes, chain operations such as Finast and the A & P are long gone from New Canaan, but the local guys made good. That's the kind of quality one gets from a market that really takes care of its customers!

A PROGRESSIVE
BUILDING COMMISSIONER

(Walter Tippman)

There was a time when New Canaan was indeed blessed to have Walter Tippman serving in the above mentioned capacity. He did so from 1946 until 1978.

Known by all as Walt, he was there when the so-called "Harvard Five" architects built homes in the town. These architects include Philip Johnson. His glass house still exists out on Ponus Ridge Road.

Architects agree that these houses couldn't have been built without the sanction of Walt. He felt that the architects knew more than he did. He let them (to borrow a late 1960's phrase) "do their thing" when it came to design & structure. Walt approved everything from foundations, both electrical & plumbing, & zoning concerns.

The modern architecture was indeed innovative. These included the houses of John M. Johansen, Richard & Geraldine Hodgson, & Eliot Noyes, as well as Hugh Smollen's pair.

But there were many detractors as well on the local level. Many residents wanted these modern architects to take their "ugly boxes" elsewhere. One went so far as to write in a letter to the editor of the *"New Canaan Advertiser"* that they "have graciously condescended to settle here & ruin the countryside with packing boxes.... An architectural form as gracious as Sunoco service stations". But Walt insisted that "we can't thwart progress".

When the "Harvard Five" built these homes property values in New Canaan were far less than they are today. Not all of these homes survive. A few have been redesigned by new owners so they can never be restored to what they once were. Fortunately Johnson's glass house survives intact.

When my high school class held their 50th reunion in October, 2013, I drove by where my parents used to live on South Avenue. I said to my now late wife, Nan, that "if you look on the left...." (whereupon I exclaimed): "Its gone!". Indeed, that nice 2 & ½ story white colonial had been razed to make room for its replacement: a "McMansion".

Walter Tippman passed away in 2010 at age 96. I wonder what he would think of these new New Canaan dwellings now.

"THE ROAR OF THE GREASEPAINT..."

(The Town Players)

One of the real highlights of my New Canaan youth was being involved with the local "amateur" theatrical company. (I put "amateur" in quotes as many professionals have been involved with it.)

BTW, the title of the this profile comes from a rather short lived Broadway musical, "The Roar of the Greasepaint & the Smell of the Crowd", by Leslie Bricusse & Anthony Newley. Though it ran for only 231 performances (starting in May, 1965), it did give the world some good songs, including "A Wonderful Day Like Today" & "Who Can I Turn To?"

Community theater has been in New Canaan since 1880, but it took until 1946 for a really permanent group to be formed. Backed by the Lions' Club, Town Players took off & is still going even stronger today.

Early productions were directed by such noted professionals as Gordon Allison, Tony Bickley (see ACTORS & ACTRESSES), & Bob Dixon. Many other professionals & former professionals have graced Town Players since then. For example, Jack Sterling turned in a most memorable performance as Professor Harold Hill in "The Music Man" late in 1963.

But many locals have participated in TP over the years. I well remember working with Hoover Sutton, Betty Mull, Nate Chatterton, Bill & Madelyn Dean, Mabel Zimmerman, Corby Lewis, Peggy Sherry, Klaus Nordling, Gretchen (Schultz) Vest, John Nickerson, & many others. They were very good to work with &

were most encouraging to me in my wanting to pursue a career as a professional actor.

One of the most memorable productions during my New Canaan years was Paul Killiam's "Next to Heaven". (See TELEVISION & RADIO to learn about Paul Killiam.) In fact, Paul wrote several such original productions for TP.

After Tony Bickley passed away in 1976, his widow wasn't sure where she was going to go next. She told TP they had to find another place to store their flats & such instead of the barn on the Bickley property. Fortunately the old Lapham estate had been turned over to the town of New Canaan. On that property stood an old powerhouse. It would take plenty of "elbow grease", but it eventually turned into the Powerhouse Playhouse. It has been home to TP since 1983.

Prior to that most auditions were held at Town Hall. Local schools opened their auditoriums for TP productions. In the early 1960's TP staged several "Off Elm" productions, which were staged in various churches.

The quality of their shows has a professional look, even better than I've seen at some professional venues. (You can't go wrong catching a show here, gang!)

"AND A BIG 'E' LIGHTS UP ON THE SCHAEFER SCOREBOARD"

(Hal Baron)

Say, gang, how many of you remember when Vin Scully used to say that during telecasts of the BROOKLYN Dodger games from Ebbets Field? The huge Schaefer Beer scoreboard adorned the right field wall of that cozy playpen many years ago.

But I'm not here to talk so much about "Dem Bums" in this profile as I am about one of their fans. In this case its Hal Baron, who was my 5th grade teacher at South School in New Canaan.

Hal was a rookie teacher during the 1955-'56 school year, but you wouldn't have known it. He was one of those rare teachers that really knew how to draw students into the lessons he taught. Several of us that had him thought he was the best elementary school teacher we'd ever had (an opinion with which this author concurs).

Hal was born & raised in the Bronx. After a stint in the U.S. Army during the Korean conflict, he went to college & earned a teaching degree. He grew up as (perish the thought!) a Yankee fan, but switched his allegiance to the flock from Flatbush years later.

Some students have various memories of him. Mark Battersby recalls him reading Charles Dickens to the class. Candis (a.ka. Candy Cousins) Kerns enjoyed Hal's stories of his personal life back then, as he used to be a musician on weekends in New York City. Patti (Liberatore) Avallone recalls "Mr. B." holding an Elvis Presley imitation contest during the 1956-'57 school year. She really liked him as a teacher, but was miffed when he wouldn't let her impersonate Elvis, as she was a girl. (That's how things were back in the conformist '50's). Patti thought this incident triggered her interest in human rights & equality.

There was a time, early in the school year, when he asked Larry Creedon to read **backwards** to the class the last sentence Hal had read to us from our textbook. Larry did so, saying: "Columbus with sailed I dreamed I night Last". We all laughed, including Hal, at this faux pas on "Mr. B.'s" part.

Were we 5th graders always angelic? Not a chance!

We were supposed to sing several songs at some assembly. One of them was "Funiculi, Funicula". Hal had to momentarily step out into the hallway to talk with some school secretary (or some such) while we had been rehearsing that song prior to the assembly. One of the girls led us in singing it this way: "Some think the world is full of alcoholics, and so do I, and so do I". We kids all chimed in & "Mr. B" came back in the room. He told us to stop that, adding (in a lighthearted, but firm, manner): "You'd better NOT sing it that way at performance!"

Hal oft times brought up current events, such as when "Ike" (a.k.a President Dwight D. Eisenhower) suffered a heart attack. We Brooklyn Dodger fans were overjoyed when the "Bums" finally won their first (&, as it turned out, only) World Series while residing in the borough of churches. He usually began the day with that & asked for our individual input on such subject matter.

I remember Hal urging us to watch the 1937 film, "Captains Courageous", when it was being broadcast on network TV. (That Spencer Tracy/ Freddie Bartholomew flick is a good one!)

Hal was a proponent of TV that educated people (this was long before PBS). He thought the program "Disneyland" could be both entertaining & informative. He applauded "Mr. Wizard". He also thought highly of Dr. Frank Baxter & the "Bell Science Series".

Then there were those trips to the Tropiquarium on the Post Road in neighboring Darien. I used to love looking at the tropical fish there, as did many of us.

Hal used to commute daily between Yonkers & New Canaan. He eventually tired of that, which is why he was at South School for a few years. He recently told me of the time when he was driving home from New Canaan on the Saw Mill River Parkway when traffic was held up for seemingly hours by a small plane that had to make an emergency landing on the Parkway.

Hal Baron is very much alive, alert & active, even though he was born in 1928. He & his lovely wife, Barbara, reside in Ardsley, NY.

THE STORY OF THE ILL-FATED BOY'S GLEE CLUB

(Self-explanatory)

The title of this "kinda/sorta" profile sounds like it could be a record done by that beloved folk group of yore, the Kingston Trio. But its not.

Return with me now to early May of 1960. We were having very nice weather then.

Ar that time New Canaan High School is where the present middle school is at South Avenue & Farm Road. There were six porticos out in front of the building.

Mrs. Jane Hilton conducted the Boys Glee Club in a few songs to start some kind of assembly, the topic of which I've long since forgotten. But then something memorable occurred.

The 18 guys in the Boys Glee Club, instead of joining us in the audience in the auditorium, had exited the stage via the rear doors. Since it was such a nice spring day, they felt exuberant. Just for kicks they carried six Volkswagen beetles from the parking lot out to the aforementioned porticos & placed them individually between the pillars.

Well, simple deduction by school officials determined it to be the handiwork of the Boys Glee Club. Each of the 18 was suspended for one week. This included the presidents of both the junior & senior class, as well as two sons of a local minister. It soon became the talk of the school.

We had gorgeous weather the following day. Many of us had spring fever. Then suddenly a fire alarm bell was sounded. Out everyone went to the grass in front of the school.

Once there several upperclassmen began ordering us to sit down. Being compliant as a freshman, I did so, as did everybody else. It was a sit-down strike in protest of the suspension of the Boys Glee Club. We stayed put for probably 20 minutes or so, lying on the grass & basking in the sun. Finally, they herded us back in.

It happened again later that day ~~~ & it happened again the next day. Rumors began flying that both print & TV media were coming out of New York to cover all this. (They didn't.) But since the weather was so gorgeous, none of us minded getting out of class.

Finally school officials had the president of the senior class come in the day after that. He was pressured into apologizing over the PA system, displaying so-called remorse for the actions of the Boys Glee Club. The suspensions stood & school life returned to normal. No more false alarms were pulled.

And that, gang, was my first taste of '60's activism.

"WAY DOWN EAST"

(Paul Brooks)

Hey, gang, how many of you recall seeing the Paul Killiam TV series, "Silents Please"? On one edition of his show, Paul Killiam screened the D.W. Griffith silent classic, "Way Down East". True, it was melodrama, but is famed for actor Richard Bathelmess hopping on the ice floes on the Connecticut River to rescue Lillian Gish, who was lying supposedly unconscious on one of the floes. (This was filmed in 1920, sans stunt people. The two stars actually did this. NO "trick photography" was involved.)

Speaking of down east, let's talk about another Paul ~~~ namely, Paul Brooks. He taught math for many years at NCHS. And yes, he was a "down easterner", hailing from Maine.

I never had him for a teacher, but he was well regarded. One of my classmates, Gretchen (Schultz) Vest, had this to say about him: "(He) was the perfect teacher for me. Math was not my best subject, but he was the most understanding & patient of any math teacher I've had before or since. (He was) a true teacher!".

Paul loved talking in his down eastern manner, explaining to students how people from Maine dropped their "r's" when speaking. He was fond of saying: "When I say propa fohm, I mean propa fohm!"

"God rest ye merry, gentleman."

"EVERY PERSON HAS A NOVEL IN HIM"

(Matt Coyle)

I'm sure Matt Coyle wouldn't mind me revising his above quote to "them" instead of "him".

Of the four English teachers I had at NCHS, I liked Matt the best. He possessed a genial countenance that made you feel welcome. He taught us expository writing & was very encouraging to young writers such as myself.

Though relatively short of stature, he nevertheless served as a Colonel in the U.S. Marine Corps during World War II. But his overall manner didn't make us think of him as a Marine, even though he could be quite firm when need be with his students.

During our junior year he had us read "Ethan Frome" by Edith Wharton, as well as Dickens' "Great Expectations" & Thoreau's "Walden". He encouraged critical thinking in the classroom discussions of these classics. He believed words conveyed real messages to the reader.

Remember *The Spectator*, gang? This annual featured short stories, essays, & poetry as furnished not just by NCHS students, but those from other high schools as well. Matt served as faculty advisor for this publication for many years.

Several of my teachers when I went to college thought I possessed the author's style of writing. I owe much of that to the fine teaching of Matt Coyle. (He passed away in 1995.)

"KEEP A SONG IN YOUR HEART"

(Jane Hilton)

Mrs. Jane Hilton had included that in her concluding sentence when she signed my senior yearbook. That's advice I seem to have kept all these years, thankfully.

Choraleers was the rather large singing group at NCHS back in the day. It consisted of 88 members my senior year, which was just under 10 % of the student population of that time. It was led by Jane. (Many of the people profiled in this book were members of it.)

I'm sure many of us enjoyed singing our way through first period, which is what we did. Jane was a fine choral director & very much the mother figure.

Choraleers put on two annual concerts. We did one at Christmas & another to welcome Spring. Lynne Hugo had much to say about one such concert:

"(F)or a Christmas concert we processed into the auditorium, all of us in robes & carrying candles, singing a capella: 'Of the Father's Love Begotten, ere the worlds began to be...'

"Mrs. Hilton stood on the stage (in front of the risers we would occupy) watching this. She stopped to exclaim: 'Oh, you kids! The music is just in you! You instinctively move to the rhythm. You're beautiful!'

"The music is in me, thanks to you who put it there. Thank you from my heart!"

Nicely said, Lynne.

We sang Christmas songs that were Christian, even though there were Jewish members of Choraleers. These included such standards as "Carol of the Bells" & "Gentle Jesus, Meek & Mild". We processed into the auditorium one particular night singing "I Heard the Bells on Christmas Day".

There was one Christmas concert during which the Girls' Glee Club sat in the front section of the auditorium. They sang the questioning refrain: "Who is this King of whom ye proudly sing?" to us Choraleers onstage. We answered them by further questioning them: "Know ye not the Christ, Jesus the Saviour?" It was most effective.

Come Spring & the music was more secular. True, we did do "O Clap Your Hands" & "Ave Maria", in addition to Franz Schubert's "Du Bist Die Ruh". We also did "Make a Joyful Noise to the Lord" (Psalm 100).

By then yours truly was a member of the Rovers, which became the name of the Boys' Glee Club following the famed VW's on the portico incident. We sang "Cindy" ("Get along home, Cindy, Cindy...") & "Sophomoric Philosophy", among other tunes, at one Spring Concert.

At one such concert Jane let various individuals step forth from the risers & solo. Sticking out in my mind were Don Mitchell's rendition of "Maria" (from "West Side Story"); Helen Croyle's memorable "Smoke Gets in Your Eyes"; Mary Powell singing "All My Trials, Lord"; & both Rick Larcom & Randy Packard performing the folk song, "Come All Ye Fair & Tender Maidens".

Jane had a tendency to worry prior to our concerts. We could see it all over her face. Yet, in performance, "All's Well That Ends Well".

One had to audition to get into Choraleers. I was indeed privileged to have been a part of it.

1962 Choraleers Christmas Concert

"SHE'LL START UPON A MARATHON & RUN AROUND YOUR BRAIN"

(Catherine Howard)

The above title was indeed quite accurate when it came to Catherine Howard! (The title of this profile is a lyric from the song, "A Pretty Girl is Like a Melody", copyright 1919 by Irving Berlin.)

Nope, this Catherine was NOT a wife of Henry VIII of England.

This Catherine taught American History at NCHS my junior year.

I was mistakenly assigned to a Basic U.S. History class to start my junior year. The teacher, Blaine Leighton, said my name was NOT on his list. So he called the school office. Turns out I was to be in Miss Howard's Academic class. Blaine's eyes lit up when he quietly said to me: "Wait'll you see Miss Howard!"

Catherine dressed conservatively, but she had an hourglass figure that most women would kill for. Skirts & dresses were knee length back in the early 1960's, but she also had very shapely legs.

Now, ladies, before you start saying I'm just another male chauvinist pig, I'm going to talk about Catherine Howard, the person.

She was a rookie teacher fresh out of college, originally hailing from some place in New Jersey. Though not as experienced in classroom debating as fellow teacher Robert Reed was, she nonetheless encouraged classroom discussion. She was quite proficient in talking about various political scandals that occurred over the years. She particularly abhorred the Nazi regime under Adolf Hitler. She talked of Woodrow Wilson's 14 points & the subsequent U.S. rejection of his proposed League of Nations so well that she caused the late Denise Hecker to declare that she felt sorry for Wilson.

Catherine (whom some of the workers in the school office called Kay) was a genuinely nice person. I lived in my parents' house on South Avenue (corner of Crystal Street). She used to always honk her horn & wave at me as she drove by in her white convertible with the Jersey plates on it. But one thing she did say to me on a private one-to-one basis was how much she liked my writing in the term paper I did on Warren G. Harding. She was most encouraging about that.

Catherine Howard was only at NCHS from 1961 till 1963. If she's still among us, she'd be nearing 80 years old. But, Kay, if you are indeed out there & reading this, please contact me at my e-mail address at the back of this book.

"AT THE HOP"

(Phil Jones)

Remember that late 1950's hit by Danny & the Juniors, gang? I well remember "cutting a rug" with Pringle Bowman to that number. (Actually it wasn't a rug, but the wooden floor of the combination gym & auditorium of the old Saxe Junior High.)

Phil Jones taught dancing after school to we 6th & 7th graders one day a week after school. This was during the bleak winter months & it certainly helped to pass the grey days at that time of year.

Phil taught us how to dance to the popular rock tunes of that time. In those days it was done to the Lindy Hop, a carryover from the Swing era. We also learned how to slow dance, as well as waltz. ("Don't worry, guys. You won't cut your hand when you touch her shoulder blade", proclaimed Phil.) We also were taught a new dance called the Cha-cha.

And what about "The Stroll"? Who can forget that!

Unfortunately, I don't have a photo of Phil. Since this was extra-curricular, the New Canaan Public Schools no longer had any information about him. But he was a genial fun guy. (I recall he used to break the outdated 78 RPM records over the top of his head from time to time.)

If any of you readers know whatever became of Phil, please let me know on my e-mail address, which is at the back of this book. Thanks

"April Love"...."Get a Job"...."Lollipop"...."Peggy Sue"..."Silhouettes"...."Sugartime"...."Tequila"...."26 Miles"...."You Send Me".

My God, wasn't that a time!

In lieu of a photo of Phil Jones, let's settle for this pair of Saxe "cuties" (circa 1958). That's Missy Brine on the left; Claire Watson on the right. They were part of a quartet that performed the Chordettes' hit song, "Lollipop", at a talent show assembly at the old Saxe Junior High.

THE SEER WHO SAW

(Blaine Leighton)

Many of us took IR as an elective our senior year. This was International Relations, well taught by Blaine Leighton.

He opened our eyes to what all was going on in the world during the "New Frontier" days of JFK. He was indeed quite prophetic in saying that our getting involved in Vietnam would be a disaster.

Mark Battersby said of Blaine: "He encouraged skepticism about certain political myths. He was (also) a champion of **real** democracy."

Lynne Vernon-Feagans recalled that he "had us read the 'News of the Week in Review' in the Sunday (edition of) *The New York Times*." He loved getting into critical thinking with us about the international news events contained in the pages of the abovementioned. We did have many a lively debate every Monday afternoon!

Debbie (Smith) Aldrich said that "Mr. Leighton's IR (class) has stuck with me all these years". I know it has mine as well.

Blaine was appointed Assistant Headmaster (a.k.a. Principal) midway through the 1963-'64 school year. Mark Battersby thought he must have been a refreshing change for the students still there after us, even though Blaine was "notoriously indifferent to taking attendance". (Yes, he had to have been a refreshing change to those students who were at NCHS between Jim St. Clair & Blaine in that position. The individual between them was NOT universally loved!)

The eleven of us on the 50th anniversary committee for NCHS '63 had very much wanted to invite Blaine to our reunion. Unfortunately, he passed away a short time before it was to be held.

"YOU GET A ZERO FOR THE DAY"

(Jim Lewis)

A muted trumpet, followed by a piano, is heard playing the song, "Seems Like Old Times", as T.V. announcer Tony Marvin in his baritone voice proclaims:

"It's ARTHA Godfrey Time, with all the lit-tle Godfrey's" (condescendingly referring to the show's cast, per Godfrey's orders).

Yes, Jim Lewis was once employed by Arthur Godfrey on both radio & TV. Jim was the lead singer in the pop & gospel quartet known as the Mariners. They were an integrated group (two Black men & a pair of Caucasians) that became buddies while serving in the U.S. Coast Guard during World War II. They discovered a common interest in singing & thus the Mariners were formed.

Jim had the distinction of being (if I'm not mistaken here) the first Black teacher hired by the New Canaan Public Schools. He came on board in September of 1958 & I had him as my 8th grade social studies teacher. Wisely he'd gotten a teaching degree in case things went sour for the Mariners. They did in 1955, when Godfrey fired them. (This was nothing new for Arthur, as he fired singer Julius LaRosa "live" on the air in 1953.) The Mariners sang for a couple more years after their sacking, but Jim knew he had to find another profession.

Those of us who had him as a teacher thought he "was tough, but fair". He came across as very stern early on in the school year. He probably took most of us aback when, if one of us was not on the ball in answering his questions, he'd say to that individual in front of the class: "You get a zero for the day!"

Early on we not only had to memorize both the "Preamble to the Constitution" & "The Gettysburg Address", but each of us had to recite them in front of the class. I was still a long way from any aspiration to becoming a professional actor & I was intimidated by this, as I'm sure many others were. Yet we persevered.

But as time went on Jim got us involved in critical thinking with some lively classroom discussions. When one of our early moon shots failed, one male student piped up with: "But we only missed the moon by three degrees". Jim's response were two emphatic questions: "Three degrees!!? Do you know how far off three degrees is in outer space!!?"

Another time we got talking about the politics of the Cold War between the Soviet Union & the United States. One brave student challenged Jim as to what he would do to try & pacify such tensions: "First of all I'd put both President Eisenhower & Premier Nikita Krushchev on a deserted island. I'd take away 'Ike's' golf clubs & Krushchev's vodka. Then they'll talk!" (He smiled as he said this & we all laughed.)

On February 3, 1959, a small plane carrying Rockers Buddy Holly, Ritchie Valens, & J.P. ("The Big Bopper") Richardson crashed in an Iowa cornfield, killing all three as well as the pilot. The next day Jim did console his stunned students quite well, but also added that (as a singer himself) he deliberately avoided flying in those one-engine airplanes.

Jim did give the students a real treat at an assembly one day. He brought back his group, the Mariners, to give a concert at an assembly. They were even better in person than on T.V.!

A real good guy was he!

That's Jim Lewis on the upper left in this group shot of the Mariners.

EXPECT THE UNEXPECTED

(V. Edgar Lind)

Edgar Lind taught chemistry at NCHS from 1944 till 1968. If you glance at his photo herein, you'd think he was a fugitive from Spike Jones & His City Slickers (that wild band that literally destroyed music in the 1940's & '50's).

Lee (Coombs) Benjamin told me of the time when Edgar casually opened class. He was talking about something besides what was in a beaker when ~~~ POOF! ~~~ the contents of the beaker exploded. He had pre-planned this, as Lee said everyone else in the classroom was startled, but not Mr. Lind.

Early on in my quartet of years at NCHS, a couple of upper-classmen guys told me that Edgar made coffee in class, using beakers & a Bunsen Burner. His students weren't always sure what to expect.

Was I somewhat that way when I taught social studies at Tonawanda High School in the suburbs of Buffalo? Let's ask two of my former "good & faithful students", Heather (Goulding) Maxwell & "Chuck" Gilbert:

Chuck: "Hey, Heather, do you remember that dude called Mr. Hahn?"

Heather: "Mr. Hahn, Mr. Hahn?.....OMG, yes! He was so BORING he'd pep up a party by leaving it!"

Moving right along I never had V. Edgar Lind as a teacher. But those who did thought he really knew his stuff when it came to chemistry.

Perhaps as Steve Martin & Dan Aykroyd used to say on "Saturday Night Live": he was a "wild & crazy guy!"

More importantly he was a good guy.

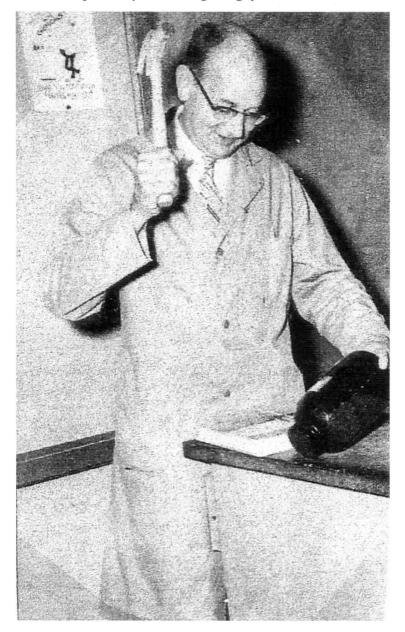

ON THE ROCKS

(William Page)

While we guys thought the aforementioned Miss Howard was gorgeous, some of the girls thought same of William Page. He taught both science & math at NCHS.

I had him for algebra & geology. He was a nice guy & a good teacher.

Geology as a subject was okay, although as a sophomore I let my homework ride oft times in that class. William chided me by saying: "If you did your homework with as much enthusiasm as you do socializing & selling yearbooks, you'd be a high honors student".

William Page was only at NCHS as long as I was (1959-1963). I have no idea what has become of him since then. (If anyone does know his present whereabouts, please email me at the address provided at the back of this book. Thanks)

A PROPHET WITH HONOR

(Robert Reed)

"Cousin Willie & Cousin Nicky".

So did Robert Reed refer to Kaiser Wilhelm II & Tzar Nicholas II.

This was during my Modern History course at NCHS my sophomore year, which was taught by Mr. Reed.

Both the Kaiser & the Tsar were indeed related to each other, as were many other European royals of that time. It was such inter marrying among royals that caused Tsarevich Alexei (Nicholas' son) to be a hemophiliac.

Mr. Reed, like the aforementioned Hal Baron, had the knack of drawing students into lessons. NCHS was indeed blessed to have some truly fine social studies teachers back in the early 1960's. Indeed, Richard Cressy, the gorgeous Catherine Howard, Art Lane, & Blaine Leighton were a great influence on me to eventually teach that subject at both the middle & high school levels.

What set Robert apart, though, was his practice of critical thinking, which led to many a classroom debate. For instance, we were talking about the collapse of some European governments & monarchies.

"That'll never happen here!", piped up one male student ~~ & the debate was on!

In an orderly fashion that statement was bantered back & forth. Mr. Reed interjected by saying: "Suppose a demagogue gets elected President of the United States. What then?" Again some students echoed the male student that started the whole ball rolling in the first place. But Mr. Reed flatly stated that dictatorships often start in the guise of democracy.

Robert tried to get Alexander Kerensky to come speak to us in class. Kerensky was the head of the provisional government in Russia between the reign of the Tsar & the Bolshevik takeover. Kerensky was 80 years old by then & living (I believe) in Westchester County, But ill health prevented him from coming to speak to us of those revolutionary days.

Robert did say that by the year 2000 you'd be able to fly all the way from Washington, DC, to Boston & see nothing but a sea of lights at night. That whole area could possibly be considered to be a megalopolis, he told us.

Don't know about the rest of my fellow students, but I nearly always left Mr. Reed's classes with my mind still focused on what all took place in his classroom. That, to me, epitomizes a good teacher.

"WHY SHOULD A GEEK LEARN HOW TO SPEAK LATIN & GREEK....?"

(Jim St. Clair)

I'm sure Jim St. Clair didn't teach his classes at NCHS to the tune of that old chestnut, "The Varsity Drag", by the 1920's songwriting team of DeSylva, Brown, et Henderson, the introduction to which I paraphrased in the title of this profile. (Yeah, gang, you can see that song sung & danced by June Allyson & Peter Lawford ~~~ yes, THE Peter Lawford ~~~ & the ensemble in the 1947 movie musical, "Good News".)

Jim has had a truly interesting teaching career. He is still very much active today. (More later.)

He has roots in both colonial New England & Cape Breton, Nova Scotia. He was born & raised in Lynn, MA, & earned his B.A. in Latin & English from Harvard in 1953. He earned his Masters degree from Harvard in 1954.

He was serving as Assistant Director of the Gaelic College of Celtic Arts in Cape Breton when then New Canaan School Superintendent Albert Mathers brought him aboard to Teach Latin, beginning that September of 1955. He was hired & brought aboard as one of four new teachers at NCHS at that time, the others being Warren Allen Smith, Elizabeth Tribble, & Stanley Twardy.

The students responded quite favorably to Jim.

He praised the diversity of the many extra-curricular activities at NCHS, feeling that this was one of the few school districts with so much cultural variety. Having performed at Harvard in plays done in both English et Latin, he was a natural when it came time to direct class plays.

He directed four such productions during the quartet of years I was at NCHS: "Don Quixote"; "Ondine"; "A Connecticut Yankee in King Arthur's Court"; & the trio of one-acters that we seniors did in "3 by '63". It was during "A Connecticut Yankee" that then senior Bob Bach ad-libbed the line upon briefly looking over old Camelot: "What is this place? Darien?"

Jim, in addition to his fine work directing such productions, also taught early morning classes in Greek, oft times at the home of Norman Cousins out in Silvermine. He did this for several years. (They also met in the NCHS cafeteria prior to the school day beginning.)

Jim served as Assistant Headmaster at NCHS from September, 1958, till June, 1962 (although in his correspondence with me he referred to the post as "principal", as did most of the student body). He eventually succeeded Harold S. Kenney as Principal when Mr. Kenney retired. Jim held that post for 3 years, including the first year at the new campus located in Waveny Park (nee the Lapham estate).

But he tired of strictly administrative work & resigned that position & moved to Mabou, Nova Scotia. There he taught as a tenured professor at Cape Breton University in Sydney for 7 years. He also taught both English & History at Mabou High School for 11 years.

Today Jim St. Clair remains most active. He resides in his great-grandparents home in Mull River, Mabou. He has written 5 books on the history, architecture, & culture of Cape Breton. He still writes a weekly column for a local newspaper & does a weekly broadcast on CBC radio, as he has done now for more than 30 years.

He has been active in both establishing & governing museums, a Center for the Arts, & a regional drama association.

Jim did Saturday school activity at NCHS to encourage students in a time of political unrest. He "kinda/sorta" participated in the "walk out" by NCHS students in protest of the Vietnam War years ago. He sat eating his bag lunch as he lounged on the grass in front of what is now Saxe Middle School. After 30 minutes he stood up & said that "I think I'll go back inside", whereupon (Jim wrote me) "mirabile dictu", the students followed (me) in & went back to their (respective) classes".

Student Director and Director
Oh, Mr. St. Clair, it can't be that bad!

(Student director Betsy Reid with Jim St. Clair
during rehearsals for "A Connecticut Yankee....")

"SIX GREY GEESE BY THE GREEN GRASS GRAZING"

(Rose Sasanoff)

Some thoughts while I ponder whatever became of Mike Leonard, Nancy Rothmayer, & "Tizzie" Sturges:

All three of the abovementioned were fellow members of the NCHS Dramatics Club. I did not join it until after I performed in my junior class play, "The Madwoman of Chaillot".

The abovementioned title to this profile is one of the many tongue twisters Rose Sasanoff threw at us to improve our diction. She taught us much about performing & developing the characters we'd portray. She & her Dramatics Club associate, Peggy Sherry, were both very active in Town Players. Being a teenager then, I wasn't always serious ~~~ usually far from it. Yet the training we received from Rose & her assistant, Peggy Sherry, did help prepare me for a "go" at professional acting.

Learning the tricks of the trade was easy for me, as well as some others. The key in professional theater is survival. There you need (as Malcolm Black, a teacher at the American Academy of Dramatic Arts when my wife Nan & I went there, put it): "the hide of a rhinoceros & the soul of a child".

Rose was a native of Holyoke, MA, having been born there in 1917. She & her then husband, Mike Sasanoff, moved to New Canaan in the late 1950's. She eventually became an English teacher at NCHS. She both wrote & directed plays, as well as short stories & two volumes of poetry, but most of this occurred after I left New Canaan.

She invited those of us in Dramatics Club as a group out to their home on Valley Road. They were very enjoyable get togethers.

Rose Sasanoff was residing in Newtown, CT, when she passed away in 2012, less than a month shy of her 95th birthday.

DRAMATICS CLUB

Front row: Chris Sturges, Georgia Wiedeman, Tizzie Sturges, Mike Leonard, Melody Buck. Middle row: Nancy Rothmayer, Penny Austin, Preston Jones, Doria Cierebiej, Tom Launsby, Henry Richards, Chris Paynter, Connie Mortlock, Bob Peckham, Mrs. Sassanoff. Back row: Bob Brinker, Tip Boxell.

THE ACTING DIRECTOR

(Peggy Sherry)

She was one English teacher I would very much liked to have had back in the day. I always thought she was "good people".

We were about midway along in rehearsals for the junior class play, "The Madwoman of Chaillot" (pronounced as in "hi-yo"), when the teacher directing it left the school system (something very unusual to occur back then). Taking his place was Peggy Sherry.

Peggy was a refreshing change from the negativity of her predecessor as director. She kept a firm hand on the production, though, & the results showed.

Peggy loved theater ~~~ & it showed! I got to know her as a fellow member of Town Players. She was a good actress in her own right. She & fellow NCHS teacher Corby Lewis (who taught social studies) loved performing with them, as did Mabel Zimmerman, an elementary teacher at South School.

This super cocky teenager was feeling he could perform virtually any role in professional theater, but Peggy helped ground me there. She also knew the realities of that fickle profession.

I did get to talk to Peggy on the phone a month or so before our 50th reunion. We had a very nice chat. I thanked her for what she did both directing "Madwoman" & assisting Mrs. Rose Sasanoff with the NCHS Dramatics Club. She very much appreciated that Though she passed away the following year, she was very much appreciated by us!

"I ENJOY BEING A GIRL"

(Margaret Teeters)

Until Lee Coombs mentioned it to me, I'd pretty much forgotten how good the 8th grade girls chorus sounded doing that selection from the Rodgers & Hammerstein Broadway musical, "Flower Drum Song". Ms Margaret Teeters really had them singing that song very well indeed!

Margaret was a classically trained singer. In fact she won raves for her performance as Magda in Carlo Menotti's "The Consul" while she was studying for her bachelor's degree at the University of Denver in Boulder, CO. She later on sang at Carnegie Hall, the old Metropolitan Opera House, & (years later) Lincoln Center.

She came on board at Saxe Junior High in the fall of 1958, along with another singer, Jim Lewis (whom I'd previously profiled). Margaret was my Music teacher there in 8th grade. She also taught both voice & piano while at Saxe, as well as serving as choir director at the Methodist Church in town.

Teaching 6th, 7th, & 8th graders at Saxe, she conveyed a sense of joy. It definitely showed in the results produced by the Girls Chorus! She taught three part harmony to them. In fact, Lee Coombs mentioned to me that Ms Teeters had them sing "You'll Never Walk Alone" in three-part harmony. It was beautifully done!

Maryanne Chinn told me the girls liked her & affectionately referred to their glee club as "Teeters' Tweeters".

Margaret went on to earn her doctorate at Columbia University. In 1966 she began teaching Music Theory & Voice at Central Connecticut State University.

Margaret Teeters originally hailed from Portland, OR. She passed away at age 91 in 2015 shortly before her 92nd birthday.

I think back on how Margaret conducted the 8th grade girls in singing "I Enjoy Being a Girl". They were so good singing it that we boys truly enjoyed them being girls!

INTRODUCTION TO THIS SECTION

My eyes welled up & tears began running down my cheeks as I read the names of my comrades in arms on the Traveling Wall. The place was just outside the North Charleston (SC) Coliseum where this was displayed nearly two decades ago.

An African-American guy with a 173rd Airborne cap perched on his head noticed me doing this. "Its okay, man", he told me gently. "I did the same thing when I saw the actual wall in DC."

Being a Vietnam combat veteran myself, I'm going to share some of my thoughts with you. I was with "B" Company, 2/14 Infantry, of the 25th Infantry Division (1966-'67). Looking back it seems as if it were a bad dream. But reality hit home that day as I viewed the Traveling Wall.

Walter Keeran, the "lifer" sergeant that survived Korea, but lost his life early on over there. With his ever present cigar in his mouth I pictured him in civilian life looking like a big city ward politician/worker.......*Stanley Sagan* (pron "Saigon") who was a sole surviving son, but volunteered to go to 'Nam even though his brother was a KIA in December, 1965.......*Pat Gilbert* from Mineola, Long Island, who returned from R. & R. where he had called stateside & asked his girlfriend to marry him. She said "yes". Sadly, he was a KIA just days later in the field.

Lest we forget these people all had lives they wished to return to. The same is true of 2 of the 3 people I'm about to profile here.

Returning to that Wall, I did see the names of both Dave Austin & "Rit" Bickford. I knew both of them at NCHS. Hopefully, dear reader, I haven't frightened you off here. I have learned through the years to look back on these fellow soldiers the way they were in life. Such will be the case with both Dave & Rit.

Keeping a sense of humor helped get me through 'Nam. Take **Billy Butler,** for instance. Billy was in my squad. He was a little guy from Morganton, NC. He got blown up by a landmine. But when I think back on Billy, I remember how he used to "blow the mind" of our squad leader, a rather paranoid Hispanic "lifer". Billy had a grin that he often employed wherein he looked like the "cat that swallowed the canary". One day I was talking with that sergeant when Billy approached from some distance away, flashing that grin.

"He's up to something, I know he is!", proclaimed our squad leader. I was laughing on the inside.

Billy, being a short fellow, was asked by the powers that be if he'd like to be a tunnel "rat". His response to that was loud & emphatic: "Hell, NO!!!"

There were others from New Canaan that were KIA's in 'Nam, but I only wrote about the two that I once knew. My apologies to the families of other KIA's. Perhaps someone in yet another book of profiles will memorialize them.

DAVE

(C. David Austin)

Dave Austin seemed to have good fortune on his side. Throughout his brief life here on earth he always seemed to get out of tough situations. Unfortunately that didn't happen on April 24, 1967.

Dave, a 1960 graduate of New Canaan High School, was the bombardier/navigator on an F4C fighter/bomber. The plane he was on was the lead aircraft of four carrying out a mission over what was then North Vietnam. They had flown out of Thailand to bomb a five-span bridge near Hanoi, as well as an electrical transformer station some seven miles from the initial target.

But during that flight the aircraft that Dave was in was hit solidly by a flak burst. The plane disintegrated. The men on the other three planes saw two large flaming pieces of the craft, but no parachutes. The flaming wreckage exploded in a fireball upon hitting the ground.

The US Air Force listed the crew of that plane as "missing in action".

I knew the Austin family, as I'd dated Dave's youngest sister, Penny, when she was a freshman & I was a senior at NCHS. Penny was in Dramatics Club with me. They were a most pleasant family that lived out on Valley Road.

Admittedly I knew Dave only slightly at NCHS. He was a senior when I was a freshman, so it was more like "Hi" & "Goodbye" in the hallways there.

But we're here to celebrate Dave's life, with the assistance of a few of his classmates. I will say that Dave had a most visible presence at NCHS when I knew him back in the day, as he was President of the Student Council during his senior year & was also a member of the National Honor Society.. He was quite energetic. He had a cute & petite blonde girlfriend named Jan Davis, who was also NCHS '60.

DON CERULLO: "(When) we were in 5th or 6th grade....Dave showed early signs of being 'military grade material'. We both had BB guns & hence our friendship started....Dave had built a fort in his backyard. We would spend hours using our 'guns'....playing military games. At times I would spend the night at his house & the games would resume the next day..... We began to drift apart into different social groups by the time we entered (Saxe Junior High)....I was working at Pitney Bowes in Stamford in the early 1970's. I saw pictures of MIA's at lunch one day & unfortunately one of them was Dave. I'll never forget that moment in time."

BRENDA (WALKER) SWORDS: "We were co-editors of the '212 Herald' in 6th grade at Center School. I think it was a mimeographed newsletter, (as we) had no Xerox machines back then. We wrote & produced it. He was jolly & fun to work with!"

HARVEY ROHDE: "The year after our 40th reunion for the class of 1960, I got together with Bob Miller & Stu Brown for a weekend in New Canaan. We were driving in the Ford Mustang convertible I had at that time, looking at old sites (from our youth)....Bob insisted we go further on Valley Road as there was something he wanted us to see. What we saw was a plaque commemorating Dave Austin."

(BTW, I owe a debt of gratitude to **MARY ELLEN (NAYLOR) CONNELL** for her guidance in directing me to the US Defense Department's POW/Missing Personnel office in the Pentagon. Thanks again, Mary Ellen.)

C. David Austin was officially declared dead by the US government in 1978, a full eleven years after his plane was shot down. His sister, Penny, passed away from breast cancer in 2011. But I certainly felt empathy for the Austin family in the lack of closure re: this.

Continuing to celebrate Dave's life, here are two items from the 1960 *Perannos*. In the one photo it appears that Dave & Jan were going domestic at Walter Stewart's Market.

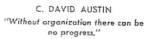

C. DAVID AUSTIN

"Without organization there can be no progress."

National Honor Society 4; Student Council (Representative) 3, (President) 4; Class Vice-President 2; Handbook (Chairman) 3, 4; Amateur Radio Club 1, 2, 3; Debating Club 4; Perannos (Layout Staff) 4; Intramurals 2, 3; Senior Play (Dr. Rezio); Junior Play (Livingston).

"I hate quotations!" . . . Advisor . . . "Take it away!" . . ."— . — ." . . .

"RIT"

(Richard Bickford)

He was known by the nickname of "Rit" during his formative years in New Canaan. He was president of both the National Honor Society & the Lettermen's Club during his senior year at NCHS. He starred in football, basketball, & baseball while a student there.

Rit went to West Point afterward, graduating there in 1967. Tragically he was a KIA in Quang Tri, South Vietnam, on October 18, 1968. His earthly remains were interred at West Point. The late Bill Saunders (NCHS '66) told me that, when he was a cadet at the Point in '68, he served as one of the honor guards when they brought Rit's coffin for burial there.

But I'm not trying to be lachrymose here. So let's remember Rit from back in the days of his youth.

Yeah, my late wife often said I "have a mind like a steel trap". I ran across a copy of the *Saxe Junior Highlights* from the spring of 1957, which I had kept (unbeknownst to me) for many years. In it was a photo taken of Rit glad handing homeroom teammate John Batty, who was crossing home plate after smacking his 3rd (or 4th or 5th) home run of a softball game at the old Saxe. The final score was something like 33-26 (or some such), with Rit's & John's homeroom winning what was apparently a real pitchers' duel.

Yep, Rit loved sports. He graduated NCHS in June of '62, but he came out with one of his wisecracks about the 1961 World Series the previous October. Cincinnati had been a surprise winner of the National League pennant that season, but I figured they wouldn't fare too well against the New York Yankees of Roger Maris & Mickey Mantle. I was right about that, as the "Bronx Bombers" dispatched them in five games. But leave it to Rit to make this poignant observation one afternoon during the Series: "Can't you just see *Pravda's* headline if Cincinnati wins it all? It'll read: 'Reds Beat Yanks!"

But now here are five of Rit's 1962 NCHS classmates to reminisce about him:

EILEEN (BAK) WROE: "I think of him often. We were in the same homeroom from kindergarten through high school. We watched each other grow up. We were friends & 'townies' together....(I) will always admire him for his greatness & his service."

BOB BACH: "(T)he event I remember about Rit was the fact that he delivered the newspapers (remember them??) early every day for Breslow's (remember them?) & that brought him to the Melba Inn (my Mom & Dad's Inn ~~ now a parking lot). Rit never passed up the opportunity for breakfast in the Inn's kitchen & my mother would frequently question me as to why I couldn't be more like Rit! Rit chided me (often) about the fact I slept too late, was frequently late for school, and therefore I would never get accepted to West Point."

"CHUCK" GRIFFITHS: "I can remember riding in the car with Rit (on the Merritt Parkway)....(H)e was sitting 'shotgun' & the song 'Runaround Sue' was playing (on the car radio), & (Rit) just started to pump his arm (to) the song....Great memories, but (now) I can't find my glasses."

GARY LIBERATORE: "After Rit's junior year his family moved to Danbury. Rit went to great lengths to make sure that we would finish his senior year at NCHS & graduate with his classmates. He moved in with the McCall family on East Avenue. The McCall's were one of the few Black families living in NC at that time. ...Rit's family had to turn over complete guardianship to the McCall's. As a fellow teammate & classmate one couldn't help but admire the way he persevered through his senior year. He was a born leader, & one who was perfectly suited for West Point & a military career."

There is a photo of Rit "kinda/sorta" embracing Gary after NCHS clinched the state championship in high school basketball in 1962. (See Gary's profile in "Sports" to view that photo.)

But this profile will close with these thoughts on Rit Bickford from another of his classmates:

CURT BRAND: "The sun was still low over the city, and the monument shadows stretched long across the ground. I was alone ~~~ just me & the Wall. I found Rit's name & the names of others I knew ~~~ young lives lost in a world away. Sadness & anger washed over me, & I cried, standing alone in the early morning light before this great black stone.

"'Where Have All the Flowers Gone?'"

"JUMPIN' JOE"

(Joe Callaway)

Fort Dix, NJ.

Early January, 1966.

Two soldiers walk toward each other during an evening's stroll. They wear their chic Army issued field jackets over their equally elegant olive drab fatigues.

The lanky redheaded fellow points at me & sez: "Wait a minute!. I know you! New Canaan, right?" We both stop & I answer him in the affirmative. We knew each other's names, even though we hadn't seen each other for a few years.

Thus it was with Joe Callaway. We both had a bit of time on our hands that evening away from our respective AIT duties, so we stopped into the nearby snack bar & had cups of coffee. The temps were above normal for that time of year, but that would soon change.

Joe & I chatted about what lay ahead for each of us. Both of us knew we were going to Vietnam. Both of us admitted we were scared. It was the classic fear of the unknown when one is about to go into harm's way. I was virtually finished with AIT while Joe still had a few weeks to go. He talked about possibly going to OCS in the unlikely chance he wouldn't get sent over there. I admitted I'd considered that as well, but personally I just wanted to get all this behind me.

Ironically, Joe doesn't remember our meeting that way, but I do.

Now let's go further back in time, shall we?

"Jumpin' Joe."

Guys with the name of Joe seem to get nicknames. Some famous ones include "Joltin' Joe" (DiMaggio); "Vinegar Joe" (Stillwell, a US Army WWII General); "Marse Joe" (former Yankee manager McCarthy); & "Tailgunner Joe" (a derisive name for Sen. Joseph McCarthy).

Joe Callaway was given his nickname by Gary Liberatore (profiled under "Sports"). Joe loved playing basketball & Gary gave him that moniker when he kept jumping for the ball over coach Joe ("Bear") Sikorski after school one afternoon. He was in that fabled class of 1961, which Mary (Riggio) Tiani of my class described as having panache. Indeed they did!

Joe told me that he & some of his '61 buddies used to be able to get beer at Walter Stewart's Market, even though the CT drinking age is 21. The Stewart twins were in Joe's class & this way they didn't have to become "ridge runners" by "jumping the line" into nearby Westchester County, NY, where the legal drinking age then was 18. But Joe admitted he & his buddies were only 16 when they started getting beer via Stewart's Market.

He took a course in International Relations as a senior at NCHS (which I did 2 years later). His teacher was Chris ("Kit") Collier. He told Joe & the other students that the U.S. seemed to be getting into an ugly situation in Southeast Asia & that some of the guys could be going over there eventually.

Joe tried his hand at college after New Canaan, but apparently his mind wasn't on his studies. So he ended up being drafted.

Joe graduated OCS in June of '66 & was promptly assigned to the 9th Infantry Division in Vietnam. He served as an infantry platoon leader for his first 6 months "in country". Joe said of those six months that was "the napalm strike right in the middle of my life". (I'd beaten him over there by 2 months, having arrived in Cu Chi with the 25th Infantry Division from Schofield Barracks on Oahu that April.)

After six months Joe was reassigned to work with US Special Forces in Thailand. He was there to help train Thailand's Queen Cobra Regiment for their eventual deployment to 'Nam. After that he volunteered to be with the 5th Special Forces in 'Nam & made a quintet of parachute jumps into unsecured landing zones. He was promoted to Captain just prior to leaving 'Nam to go "back to The World" (as we G.I.'s then referred to the U.S.A.).

Joe has detailed much of his New Canaan life, as well as his time in Vietnam, in the book he authored titled "Mekong First Light". He also talked at length about the problems Vietnam veterans faced after their return home.

Of his book, one sergeant said: "(T)he troops all thought you'd be the first lieutenant killed, and in the end, you were the only one left. We were all wrong. You were the best."

Another enlisted man said of Joe: "LT Callaway led us for six months with his professionalism & smart decision making. I will forever be grateful for his leadership getting us through such a difficult time in our lives. This book has helped me to come to terms with my experience, which has been very difficult to talk about....Once you pick up this book, you will never put it down.".

Joe completed his college education at Boston University in 1972. Today he is retired from work in the private sector & resides with his wife, Susan, in Danville, CA. They have three sons & six grandchildren (two of the latter are pictured below along with Joe & Susan).

Thankfully both Joe & I returned home safely to tell about it.

NOTHING TRIVIAL ABOUT HER

(Ann Curry)

Say, gang, here's a good trivia question to ambush your friends with: Everyone is familiar with the NBC chimes. What three musical notes are played on that? (The answer appears at the end of this particular profile.)

As I wrote above, there is nothing trivial about Ann Curry. In this day & age when some of these political clowns scream "fake news", Ann is a real journalist.

Born in Guam in 1956, she has literally (as John Cameron Swayze used to say) "hopscotched the world" to do news stories. She was on site after the tsunami that devastated Southeast Asia, as well as the 2010 earthquake that leveled much of Haiti. She's been on the scene covering numerous wars, including Iraq & Afghanistan among many other hot spots. (Ann did all this for NBC.)

When it comes to her ethnic background, she is definitely diverse. Her father was from Colorado; he is of Cherokee, French, German, Scottish, & Irish descent. Her mother is Japanese. Ann's dad was a U.S. Navy sailor who met her mom when she was a street-car conductor during the U.S. occupation of Japan following World War II.

Ann is a 1978 graduate of the University of Oregon's School of Journalism. She worked as a reporter & eventual news anchor at TV stations in Oregon as well as Los Angeles. She joined NBC news in 1990. She eventually worked her way up the ladder to become the "Today Show" news anchor from 1997 till 2011. She had the second longest tenure as a news anchor on that program, surpassed only by the late Frank Blair, who did those honors from 1953 until 1975. Ann was the principal substitute as "NBC Nightly News" anchor from 2005 until 2011. Originally co-hosting "Dateline NBC" with Stone Phillips from 2005 till 2007, she became sole host of that program from then on until she joined Matt Lauer as co-host of the "Today Show" in June of 2011.

On December 17, 2007, Ann bungee jumped from the Transporter Bridge in Manchester, England. She did this to raise money for charity. That event was covered live on the "Today Show". (Oh, well. To each their own.)

This writer is not at all sure what led to her departure from "Today" just a year after she was selected as co-anchor. It has been rumored that she & Lauer didn't get along with each other. But Ann stayed on at NBC News until she resigned from it in January, 2015.

Ann Curry is still very much active on TV, doing the series "We'll Meet Again" on PBS. This program looks at the lives of ordinary people caught up in (& later reunited) after being through some historic events in both this century & the last one.

(Oh, yes: the answer to that trivia question are the notes G-E-C. General Electric had much to do with the founding of NBC back in the mid-1920's.)

A "MURROW BOY" MAKES GOOD

(Douglas Edwards)

May, 1945.

A young Douglas Edwards sits alongside famed broadcaster Edward R. Murrow in a radio studio in London. Londoners were jubilant as World War II in the European Theater was over.

"Well, Ed", began Douglas, "on this great **VD** ~~~ I mean, VE Day in London...."

By then, the usually somber Murrow was crouched beneath the desk the two shared on air, trying to contain himself from laughing too loudly as Douglas continued with the news of that event for the next three minutes. (Ah, yes, the perils of "live" broadcasting.)

Most folks my age remember him as the news anchor of "Douglas Edwards with the News" on CBS T.V., a post he held from 1948 until April, 1962. He had a long & distinguished career with that network on both radio & T.V.

Douglas was born in Ada, OK, in 1917, but raised in Birmingham, AL. He came to CBS Radio in 1942 after working as a newscaster & announcer on stations in Atlanta & Detroit. He was on CBS Radio until the 1948 political conventions came along. Some of the top journalists on CBS Radio didn't want anything to do with the newborn medium of television, but Douglas did. Thus, he was chosen to "host" the convention coverage. (The term "anchor" didn't come into being until Walter Cronkite did the honors for CBS at the 1952 conventions.)

CBS brass was impressed enough with Douglas to have him do his own 15 minute evening newscast. Thus, "Douglas Edwards With the News" came into being on T.V. His principal competition soon came from "The Camel News Caravan" with John Cameron Swayze on NBC for the next 8 years. Douglas scored a coup by flying in a helicopter to film the badly listing "Andrea Doria" by the continental shelf in the Atlantic in the summer of 1956. He broadcast from the chopper as the "Andrea Doria" sank beneath the waves following its collision with fellow luxury liner, the "Stockholm" (the latter making it safely to port in New York).

But after Chet Huntley & David Brinkley replaced Swayze, Edwards' ratings began going down. In April of 1962 the aforementioned Cronkite succeeded Douglas in the anchor chair. By September of the following year the newscast was expanded to 30 minutes & renamed "The CBS Evening News".

Douglas stayed active in broadcasting after that, but primarily as a radio journalist, until his retirement in 1988. On occasion he came on TV to do a daytime one minute-plus news summary during the 1980's.

But what of Douglas Edwards, the person?

His youngest daughter, Donna (Edwards) Brinckerhoff, told me the family moved to New Canaan from nearby Weston in 1966. By then all three Edwards children had grown up. Douglas & his wife purchased a home on Turtleback Road that already had a crown-shaped swimming pool in place. Donna said he loved entertaining his three adult children & the grandchildren by poolside.

Although he truly loved doing his journalistic endeavors, It seems that Douglas lived for weekends. He loved to stroll about town, taking in the fresh air & the still country-like quality that New Canaan then had. He enjoyed playing tennis as well. He shopped for steaks at Gristede's on Elm Street in the center of town & "charred them beyond recognition" on his grill, according to Donna. His daughter also said he was a real "foodie", as he enjoyed dining out in such places as Savelle's Chicken (followed by a sundae at Baskin Robbins); the Roger Sherman Inn; & Emily Shaw's (the last named located in neighboring Pound Ridge, NY), among other establishments.

Douglas gave back to the community as well, doing fundraisers & benefits. He also did pro bono talks at nearby colleges & institutions. Turtleback Road neighbor Jack Sterling of CBS Radio quite often accompanied Douglas on such ventures.

But then Monday morning rolled around. The reverie of the weekend was replaced by the reality of work, although he truly loved doing his journalistic endeavors.

Douglas Edwards passed away in Sarasota, FL, in 1990, a scant two years into his retirement.

THE "TRIB"

(Joseph Herzberg)

"Who says a good newspaper has to be dull? I read the *Herald Tribune.*"

So said that advertising slogan of yore about that daily New York City newspaper. Joe Herzberg worked for that fabled newspaper from 1925 till 1956. He was a neighbor of mine, living katy-cornered across South Avenue from me.

Joe loved New York. He was born in the Bronx on New Year's Day in 1907, but it was Manhattan which drew him like a magnet. He began with the "Trib" as a copy boy just after his 1925 graduation from high school. He eventually worked his way up through the ranks, serving as a reporter, rewriteman, assistant editor, city editor, & Sunday editor. (He collaborated on a book, "Late City Editon", in the late 1940's about doing just that with the "Trib".)

If one were to go to central casting for a care-worn newspaper editor, Joe would have been the perfect choice. He definitely looked the part, with the stooped shoulders & the cigarette dangling from his lips. He had the requisite bags under his eyes as well.

As stated earlier, he fell in love with Manhattan. He frequented such theaters as the Palace, the Paramount, & the Roxy. Being a newspaperman he loved tipping a few in various saloons. He loved chatting with people when he was off-duty. He often went to the Polo Grounds to see his beloved Giants play beneath Coogan's Bluff. He used to reminisce about the glory days of that team under the tutelage of John McGraw. He was so fascinated by baseball that he told me shortly before the team fled west to 'Frisco that Daryl

Spencer couldn't hold a candle to Travis Jackson when it came to playing shortstop.

The *Herald Tribune* was very much an eastern (a.k.a. moderate) Republican newspaper. It's scope was international as well. The "Trib" had many fine columnists during Joe's days there, including Jimmy Breslin, Art Buchwald, Judith Crist, Walter Kerr, Walter Lippman, "Red" Smith, & Dorothy Thompson, among others. The paper catered to the suburban crowd.

But the "Trib", though in direct competition with the prestigious *New York Times*, had their financial woes as well. The Reid family of Westchester County owned the paper for seemingly ages. Eventually they sold it to the Whitney family, who made some sleeker changes to the paper, starting shortly their 1958 purchase of it. These included that column on the left hand side of the front page with the "slug": "In the News This Morning", which gave capsulized summaries on the news events contained on the pages therein. In the early 1960's an associate editor named Clay Felker created a magazine section for the Sunday edition with the simple title of **New York**. Once the "Trib" folded in 1966 (due to numerous newspaper strikes in the 1960's), Felker carried on with that publication as a successful separate entity.

But Joe was long gone by then, switching over to the *Times*. He long had a reputation as a workhorse, putting in (as one colleague said after Joe died) "27 hours a day". At the *Times* he became that newspaper's first cultural news editor, a post he held until his retirement in 1970.

I was friends with his son, Paul, back in the day. Joe's wife, Marion, predeceased him by nearly a dozen years. She & my mother,

Louise B. Hahn, worked together in the Superintendent's office of the New Canaan Public Schools for several years.

Joe Herzberg passed away just before Valentine's Day in 1976 at age 69.

Joe Herzberg in 1947.

"IS IT TRUE WHAT THEY SAY ABOUT (THE) DIXIE (CATS)?"

(The Dixie Cats)

I'd first heard the Dixie Cats perform during an assembly at Saxe Junior High during the spring of 1957 when I was in 6th grade. The sextette was comprised of 8th graders. They were quite good! (The above song, BTW, was copyrighted in 1936 by composers Irving Caesar, Sammy Lerner, & Gerald Marks.)

The dixieland jazz group was formed by Frank ("Sandy") Hermes & the late Pete Freeman. The group could have been known as Bob & Pete & Paul & Pete & Sandy & Pete, but they wisely opted for the Dixie Cats instead.

The group consisted of Paul Chipello on piano, Freeman played the sax, Pete Ward displayed his talent on the trumpet, Pete Vernon was the clarinetist, Bob Stark kept rhythm with the drums, & Sandy (a.k.a. Max) emulated Tommy Dorsey with the trombone. They definitely made us tap our feet.

Sandy said they got gigs all over Fairfield County & were well compensated, despite being in their teens. On occasion they had to transport a piano for Paul in a pick-up truck. But their music was well received wherever they played. Their gigs included receptions in private homes.

The Dixie Cats became a septet during their senior year at NCHS (1960-'61) with the addition of one of my classmates, Joe Boccuzzi, on bass fiddle.

Much like the NCHS rock group, the Earles, the Dixie Cats broke up after finishing high school. But one of their members gained some notoriety in the music business down the road. That was pianist Paul Chipello.

Paul had taken piano lessons with Sister Rita of St. Aloysius Church when he was very young. He earned an electrical engineering bachelor's degree at Villanova, but soon felt he didn't belong in big business. So he chucked that career & began accompanying the group, the Lettermen, in the late 1960's. He was doing what he loved doing best.

Later on he became a freelance musician in Los Angeles, playing piano at corporate events & private parties. He also taught piano & arranged music for musical theatre.

He was charitable when it came to helping build houses for Habitat for Humanity, among other such causes. He served as a Deacon in his L.A. church.

Sadly, Paul Chipello passed away on Christmas Day, 2014, at age 71.

Dixie Cats, Left to Right: Paul Chipello, Pete Freeman, Pete Ward, Pete Vernon, Bob Stark, Frank Hermes.

WHEN ROCK WAS YOUNG & INNOCENT

(The Earles)

Hey, gang, remember back in the day was Rock 'n Roll was new ~~~ I mean REALLY new?

That was when some extreme adults literally screamed that such music was the work of the devil & a communist plot! (Lighten up, adults.)

But New Canaan High School produced some rock bands back then. One of the best was the Earles.

This group was formed by Dave Loomis & John Poole, both from the class of 1964. In fact most of the band came from that class, with the exception of Bill Warren (1963). But let's hear how John Poole described things:

"That certainly was a great period. Full of innocence & good feelings to all we touched, & a great group of band mates ~~~ Loomis, Warren, (the late) Robbie Weed, Bob Dix, Stan Duffendack, and Bob Monaco. I recall with great fondness driving back from gigs late at night in Dave's '56 Merc & all of us very happy from a successful performance in places like Mount Kisco, & as far out as East Hampton on Long Island!"

Warren played guitar & also the electric piano. Loomis & Poole were guitarists; Weed was the drummer; & both Dix & Monaco played sax, with the former doubling on trumpet when needed.

Poole went on to say: "(W)e created great music for all our high school friends. We never hurt anyone, never drank too much, never sexually assaulted anyone."

The Earles' repertoire included the classic Ray Charles hit, "What'd I Say?". As well as such songs from a quartet from Liverpool titled "I Wanna Hold Your Hand" & "She Loves You".

But with the arrival of the Beatles came a signal that things were changing in the music scene. There would be no more sayings by teens such as: "Hey, its got a good beat & you can dance to it".

As Poole concluded: "(T)hat was the end of an era for us.... very sadly....but we all realized we had to move on".

Their timing of when they were a group was indeed fortuitous for the teens of New Canaan. They were a good group & a breath of fresh air.

Thanks for the memories, guys!

Front row (l to r): Dave Loomis & Bill Warren.

Back row (l to r): John Poole, Robbie Weed, & Bob Dix

"AND ALL THAT JAZZ"

(Jeff Fuller)

The relaxing low-key Brazilian jazz sounds were heard throughout much of the lobby in the new Sheraton Hotel in Stamford that mid-October Friday night in 2013. The small combo was called Sambaleza and was led by Jeff Fuller.

The occasion was the kick-off of the 50th reunion of the NCHS class of 1963. It was "Meet & Greet" for many of us, nearly all of whom I hadn't seen since we graduated. The music was in the background, but my classmates enjoyed it. It wasn't so loud that you couldn't talk over it. I stopped and listened to it a couple of times. Ray Burghardt (profiled under "THE WORLD STAGE") was sitting there really drinking in the music while we chatted briefly.

Jeff is going to tell you much about himself here while I again take a brief "R. & R.":

"I was born in North Woodstock, CT, in 1945. I was 3 years old when my family moved to the Silvermine area of New Canaan. My father was a writer and he found work in the burgeoning TV industry. I attended public schools all the way through high school. At South School my friends included Candy Cousins, Margot Eberman, Randy Packard, Claire Watson, and many more. Steve Roos ~~ who later went away to private school ~~ ended up as my college roommate many years later at Yale.

"New Canaan High School was a lot of fun. I studied hard and did well in all my classes except English, where I could rarely sit still long enough to complete reading assignments and the ensuing reports which were due. I loved the athletics at NCHS. I ran track for a bit, was manager of the football team, and played basketball all four years. Our basketball team ~~ under the leadership of captain Gary Liberatore (profiled in "SPORTS") ~~ won the CT

State Championship in 1962, beating undefeated Plainville in the last seconds.

"The excellent academic preparation at NCHS allowed me to get into Yale on early decision at the end of my junior year in high school. I decided to major in Music my sophomore year ~~ a decision I have never regretted. I took every undergrad music class Yale offered ~~ history, theory and composition. I studied piano privately, and learned guitar: classical, jazz, & rock. I earned a Master's in Composition from the Yale School of Music.

"In 1967 I met the woman who has been in my life ever since: Pamela Saffer, my partner then and my partner today. Though we never married, I couldn't have gotten this far in life without her. We still maintain a healthy relationship and, more importantly, a healthy friendship in our 52nd year together. The adventures of our lives could fill a book, but suffice it to say that, though we have spent time both together and apart, we have grown up together.

"There came a time, roughly 1974, when I started playing jazz on the upright bass, and I have continued doing that professionally to this day. I have been fortunate to play with many well-known jazz artists. Eventually I joined NEA Jazz Master Lou Donaldson's band and I performed and toured with him for more than 15 years. I lived in Manhattan most of this time.

"At a jam session in a Havana nightclub I met the great Cuban saxophonist Paquito D'Rivera. Soon after I was a member of Paquito's combo, where I really cut my teeth learning both Cuban and Brazilian music.

"Eventually New York City and touring wore me down a bit and I moved back to New Haven in 1986. I continued to perform, compose, and record, but I also began teaching extensively at (both) the high school and college levels. These days I'm back at Yale University as an adjunct instructor in jazz. I have a small record company and have recently put out 4 CD's of mostly my own original compositions with my own trio. Please check out my website at www.jefffuller.net."

Thanks, Jeff, for the brief respite.

Oh, yes: the title of Jeff's profile is the first song heard in the musical, "Chicago", which was written by John Kander and Fred Ebb. (Gotta give credit where credit's due, gang.)

"STRIKE UP THE BAND!"

("Skitch" Henderson)

A quick drum roll is heard 4 times in rapid succession, after which the full orchestra chimes in with the theme that singer Paul Anka wrote for the "Tonight Show" many years ago. The camera located high above Times Square focuses in on the Canadian Club neon sign at night, then pans upward & slowly to the right. The Time-Life Building is clearly seen just before the camera settles in on 30 Rock. We hear the off-camera announcer saying:

"From New York, it's the 'Tonight Show' starring Johnny Carson.

"Please join Johnny & his guests....

"Amelia Earhart....,

"Glenn Miller....,

"and Jimmy Hoffa.

"With 'Skitch' Henderson & the NBC Orchestra....

"And me, I'm Ed McMahon.

"And now,...."

No, the above listing of guests never occurred. I just put all that in there to make sure you were still awake.

In addition to being an orchestra conductor, Skitch was both a pianist & composer. He was born in Minnesota in 1918 & christened Lyle. His paternal aunt taught him how to play the piano, starting at age 4. He learned the ropes of classical music under the likes of Arnold Schoenberg & Arturo Toscanini, but supported himself by playing swing music. He became known as an arranger that could "re-sketch" a song in different keys. This was what brought about the nickname of "Skitch".

After service in World War II he was musical director on radio for Frank Sinatra & served as the accompanist on "Bing" Crosby's radio show. He recorded several records with his own band for the newly formed Capitol records.

He landed a long running gig on NBC T.V., succeeding Toscanini as that network's musical director in the early 1950's. He conducted the NBC Orchestra on the versions of the "Tonight Show" that were hosted by both Steve Allen & the aforementioned Carson. (He left "Tonight" during 1966.) He also conducted that orchestra on Steve Allen's Sunday night show in the late 1950's. There was a comic side to Skitch & he proved that by sometimes appearing on the recurring comedy skit entitled "The Man on the Street" interviews. One Christmas he even decorated his Van Dyke beard with twinkling Christmas lights for that segment.

He also served as co-host with his then wife on "Faye Emerson's Wonderful Town". Both lived in New Canaan during the time they were married (1950-'57).

Skitch, though, did get in hot water legally & was indicted for income tax evasion in 1974. He spent four months in federal prison from April till August of 1975 for that offense.

Skitch & his wife Ruth both owned & operated The Silo, which was a well renowned store, art gallery, & cooking school located in New Milford, CT. They continued operating this until Skitch's 2005 passing.

(BTW, "Strike Up the Band" was a song written & copyrighted by the brothers Gershwin, George & Ira, in 1927.)

That's "Skitch" seated at the piano on the "Tonight Show" (1955).
Standing l. to r.: Eydie Gorme, Steve Lawrence, & Steve Allen.
(Remember the Davy Crockett fad back then, gang?)

ENCORE, MAESTRO!

(Andre Kostelanetz)

Hey, gang, remember that version of "Santa Claus is Comin' to Town" that was played upon Old St. Nick's arrival at Macy's Herald Square store? This was played annually at the conclusion of the Macy's Thanksgiving Day Parade for a good many years until recently. Though it was recorded music, it was done by Andre Kostelanetz & His Orchestra.

Frankly, I enjoy his music. I was initially exposed to it on old 78 RPM records my parents had when I was a very young kid. His album back then of Sigmund Romberg songs had a relaxing, dreamy quality to it.

Andre was born Abram Kostelyanetz in St. Petersburg, Russia, three days before Christmas in 1901 to a prominent Jewish family. His father was quite active with the St. Petersburg stock exchange & his maternal grandfather was a wealthy merchant & industrialist in the timber industry. Andre did study music when young & he preferred that to what his family did.

He fled the newly formed Soviet Union in 1922 & came to New York, conducting concerts on the radio. He received his own radio program, "Andre Kostelanetz Presents", which aired weekly during the 1930's on CBS radio. He specialized mainly in light classical music & Broadway show songs.

He met & fell in love with opera star Lily Pons, who was a coloratura soprano. They wed in 1938 & divorced 20 years later. They recorded several albums together.

Kostelanetz also commissioned many modern classical pieces, including Aaron Copland's "Lincoln Portrait"; Ferde Grofe's "Hudson River Suite"; Jerome Kern's "Portrait of Mark Twain"; & William Schumann's "New England Triptych". He also recorded many easy listening albums of pop music. (More later.) He never denied he was seeking to find a wide audience for the music he played.

He was once quoted as saying: "If I can leave an inheritance of a growing audience for the concert hall, I have accomplished everything".

IMO he did just that.

Andre Kostelanetz passed away in Port-au-Prince, Haiti, in January of 1980.

Yes, I like all kinds of music. When I'm in the mood for relaxing music I'll play CD's & LP's of such artists as Nat King Cole, Ray Conniff, Ella FitzGerald, the Kingston Trio, Henry Mancini, Glenn Miller, George Shearing, Frank Sinatra ~~~ &, of course, Kostelanetz.

I have many CD's & LP's of Andre's. These include "The Nutcracker Suite"; "Strauss Waltzes'; the music of both George Gershwin & Jerome Kern; "Wonderland of Christmas"; "New York Wonderland"; "Scarborough Fair"; "Kostelanetz Plays Hits from 'Funny Girl', 'Finian's Rainbow', & 'Star!'", "Kostelanetz Plays Cole Porter" & "Michel LeGrand's Greatest Hits". All are very much MOR & well done!

Speaking of "Christmas Wonderland", the song "Santa Claus is Comin' to Town" is on that album. So, too, is a rather unique version of Leroy Anderson's "Sleigh Ride". I love that whistling instrument Andre utilized on that number. In fact, I'm still trying to figure out just what instrument was played that achieved that effect. (He recorded that back in 1963 before the moog caught on.) If you, dear reader, have any idea just what instrument it was, please e-mail me at the address provided at the back of this book.

A DAY IN THE LIFE OF A DIVA

(Lily Pons)

Actually, it's the *years* in the life of a diva, in this case opera coloratura soprano Lily Pons.

She was born Alice Josephine Pons in Draguignan, France (which is close to Cannes) in 1898. She sang for soldiers & played piano for them at various receptions during World War I. Following that "war to end all wars" she took formal singing lessons in Paris, as well as New York, to which she emigrated in the late 1920's.

She rapidly gained attention as a fine coloratura, enough so that she was signed on to replace Amelita Galli-Curci in 1930. She formally changed her first name to Lily when she made her debut at the Met in January, 1931. She received tremendous acclaim as Lucia in Donizetti's "Lucia di Lammermoor" at that time & became opera's newest star. (Lily performed at the old Met nearly 300 times between 1931 & 1960.)

Lily was terrific at self-promotion as well. Her countenance graced printed advertisements for Knox Gelatin, Libby's Tomato Juice, & Lockheed Airplanes. A town in Maryland was so enamored of her that they changed the name of their community to Lilypons. She even arranged to have the Christmas cards she sent annually postmarked from that town. It's been implied that her only rival for such self-promotion among opera stars came years later with Luciano Pavarotti.

She married conductor Andre Kostelanetz in 1938, two years before she became a naturalized U.S. citizen. Lily & Andre toured with the USO in 1944 in such places as North Africa, Italy, the

Middle East, India, & Burma. Andre conducted a band made up of American G.I.'s while Lily sang for the troops in those abovementioned locales. They both toured & entertained G.I.'s the following year in China, Belgium, France, & close to the action in Germany. (She & Kostelanetz divorced in 1958.)

Lily performed in many operas, among them Verdi's "Rigoletto", Rossini's "The Barber of Seville", & Offenbach's "Tales of Hoffman", to name but a few. Her final performance at the old Met came in December of 1960.

She continued doing concerts after that throughout much of the world until her formal retirement from singing in 1973. Lily Pons passed away in early 1976 at age 77.

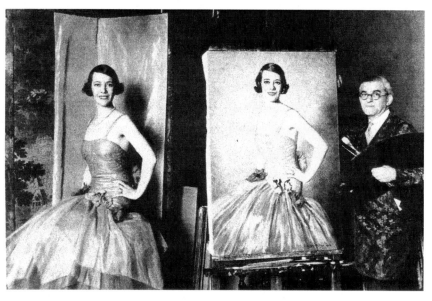

Lily having her portrait painted by an unknown artist.

"I PLAY THE ICE CUBES"

(McCoy Tyner)

Years ago comedian Sid Caesar uttered that line, probably on either TV's "Your Show of Shows" or "Caesar's Hour". He was supposed to be a hip jazz musician. When asked how it sounded to play the ice cubes, Caesar responded with: "Cool, man".

McCoy is a fine jazz pianist. He was born in Philadelphia, PA, in 1938. His mother was supposed to be his biggest influence when it came to playing the piano.

His jazz career began to get going with Benny Golson's & Art Farmer's Jazztet in 1960. Later that year he hooked up with saxophonist John Coltrane & his group. McCoy tickled the ivories on Coltrane's famed rendition of "My Favorite Things". He was heard on several albums that the Coltrane group recorded between 1961 & 1965, including: "Live at the Village Vanguard" & "Live at Birdland".

But McCoy split with Coltrane in '65. John decided to augment his quartet with percussion, which McCoy felt was drowning out his musical contributions. So McCoy formed his own jazz trio in 1966. That group produced several fine albums. Among them were: "The Real McCoy" & "Tender Moments" (both 1967); "Expansions" (1968); "Extensions" (1970); & "Enlightenment" (1973). On the 1975 album, "Trident", he played both the celeste & the harpsichord.

Jazz aficionados consider McCoy Tyner to be one of the most influential jazz pianists of the 20th century. He is still active as a jazz musician to this day.

"PLAY, PETER"

(Peter Van Steeden)

Sometimes God does move in mysterious ways.

I was seriously thinking of jettisoning a profile of Peter Van Steeden solely because I had so little information about him. Then I posted on the Facebook site, "If You're from New Canaan...", the need for photos of a few individuals. I also asked members of that site for their memories of both the Deli-Bake & Fairty's Farm. The response to that was terrific! One of those prominently featured in both is Michael Ahearn. He was kind enough to inform me that his sister-in-law is Dale (Conron) Ahearn. She is the granddaughter of Peter Van Steeden.

Dale was kind enough to provide me with a wealth of information on her grandfather. So, writing this up makes it the final profile for this book. Off we go.

Famed radio comedian Fred Allen used to introduce his radio show with the words: "Play, Peter". At this point Peter Van Steeden conducted the studio orchestra in the show's theme song.

Allen was a pioneer in bringing his orchestra leader to the forefront. This was something Steve Allen (NO relation to Fred) did with "Skitch" Henderson on TV years later & has become a tradition ever since.

Peter was born in Amsterdam, Holland, in 1904. His family emigrated to the U.S. when he was but 3 years old. Peter was a child prodigy when it came to music, however, as he was able to skillfully play the violin by the age of 6.

He had initially considered a career in Industrial Engineering. He went to NYU to study that, but got sidetracked along the way when he organized NYU's first ever band, Van & His Collegians. It was a great success & Peter later formed it into Peter Van Steeden & His Orchestra. They became a society orchestra that played in the finest supper clubs from coast to coast. They also got many gigs on network radio.

This came to Fred Allen's attention, who hired Peter in 1935. He came to the forefront on Fred's show thanks to a lousy haircut by a substitute barber. Peter's hair was sticking out weirdly & Allen quipped on the air: "Van Steeden, your hair looks like the worn-out elbow of a two dollar raccoon coat". The audience howled at this & Peter's haircuts became a recurring joke on the show.

Peter was there for the birth of "Allen's Alley". On this regular bit Allen & his real life wife, Portland Hoffa, used to figuratively stroll down the Alley, encountering such regulars as a downeasterner farmer named Titus Moody ("Howdy, bub"). Parker Fennelly played that role, while Kenny Delmar also brought down the house as the boisterous southern windbag named Senator Claghorn ("That's a joke, son.") The latter was so memorable that Warner Brothers created a cartoon character named Foghorn Leghorn based on Senator Claghorn.

Yes, Peter was definitely there for the Golden Age of network radio! He led the studio orchestra for a dozen seasons on "Mister District Attorney". He also did same for the "Lucky Strike Hit Parade" (remember the tobacco auctioneer on their ads on TV, gang? They did it on radio as well) & "Duffy's Tavern" ("Duffy's Tavern, where the elite meet to eat"). He also got in on the ground floor when television came along, most notably leading the orchestra on "Omnibus".

Peter wrote songs as well, his most famous being "Home (When Shadows Fall)". This was recorded by such artists as the Dorsey Brothers, Ruth Etting, Louis Armstrong, Nat King Cole, the Mills Brothers, Sam Cooke, Della Reese, Dean Martin, & (in 2012) Paul McCartney. Yes, he did compose many songs, but one I've yet to hear is "Home for Christmas", which contains the lyric: "...and the carol singing on God's Acre".

Peter felt right at home in New Canaan. He married his childhood sweetheart, Margery Wells. Their union produced 5 children. They (wisely) decided to move to New Canaan, setting up home on Ponus Ridge Road. Here he became very much involved with Town Players (see COMMUNITY LEADERS). He led the orchestra for literally decades whenever they put on a musical. Peter even composed the score for two of them, "Happily Ever After" & "Next to Heaven".

I knew Peter only slightly when I was a member of TP. He struck me as a reserved man that was primarily focused on the music. (Then, too, I was only in my teens then.)

Peter lost a leg as the result of an accident in the 1960's, as it was so bad it had to be amputated. But he pressed on despite this unforeseen handicap, conducting for TP for years after that happened.

His wife Margery passed away in 1974. His daughter (Margery Conron) took him in to live at their Myanos Road house. Nonetheless, he remained active in the community.

Peter Van Steeden passed away just after the New Year began in 1990. He was 85.

A WORTHY SUCCESSOR TO AARON COPLAND

(Gwyneth Walker)

Years ago I worked in Development for the Buffalo Philharmonic Orchestra. There was a woman that worked in subscription sales there that was habitually late for work.

One morning she sauntered in close to 10:30. I was speaking with her immediate supervisor about something when she approached us. He asked her why she came in so late. Her reply was one of the most original excuses I've heard for tardiness.

"Well", she stated, "last night I had a party in my apartment. I went to bed & when I awoke I discovered that my friends had tied all my underwear in knots. So I had to borrow a pair of panties from an old lady down the hall so I could come into work."

Fortunately, Gwyneth Walker is NOT like that. In fact, she is a modern classical composer similar to both the aforementioned Copland & Charles Ives.

Gwyneth is a third generation New Canaanite. Her grandparents came to New Canaan from Brooklyn Heights to establish a summer home back in the 1890's. Though born in New York City in 1947, Gwyneth was raised in New Canaan. She attended public schools in town through 8th grade before going to prep school at Abbot Academy - Phillips Academy in Andover, MA.

It was in Andover that she initially performed in vocal octets, in which she wrote all the choral arrangements. She continued doing this during her college years at Pembroke College in Brown

University & the Hartt School of Music. She earned three degrees in Music Composition.

She wed fellow composer David Burton (1945-1975) & she joined the faculty of the Oberlin College Conservatory. She decided to exit academia in order to become a full-time composer in 1982.

Through the years she has written over 300 compositions for not only orchestra & chamber ensembles, but for choruses, solo voice, & various individual instruments. These have been performed in such places as Carnegie Hall, the Washington National Cathedral, & "The Ellen Show".

Gwyneth has said that "My pieces always have melody & form & a rhythm that's right there for you". Among her most popular compositions are "Songs for Women's Voices" (which she based on poems by American poet May Swenson) & "A Vision of Hills" (which was inspired when she resided in Braintree, VT, for many years).

That last named composition is on CD. Other CD's of her works include "An Hour to Dance"; "Now Let Us Sing!"; "The Sun is Love"; & "Scattering Dark & Bright".

The Center for Catholic Studies at Fairfield University commissioned her to write "Songs to the Lord of Peace". This premiered at that CT school in April, 2007.

Other compositions include "A Heart in Hiding (The Passionate Love Poems of Emily Dickinson)"; "Across the Water"; & a new setting of the Henry Wadsworth Longfellow poem, "Paul Revere's Ride".

Gwyneth has been "Composer in Residence" with the Great Lakes Chamber Orchestra in Petrosky, MI, since 2017. She is in the process of writing a new cantata titled "The Great Lakes".

(Ah, yes. It is January as I write this. Speaking of the Great Lakes, I think back on those gentle zephyrs that come in from Lake Erie to Buffalo & environs at this time of year.)

Gwyneth Walker currently makes her home in New Canaan. She remains an avid tennis player. She was a Tournament Tennis Player in her teens in New Canaan. Wouldn't be at all surprised if two of her opponents were Gail (Davidson) Overbeck & Cathy (Eaton) Schmidt.

NOW PICTURE THIS

(Margaret Bourke-White)

She was an independent woman long before Women's Liberation.

Margaret Bourke-White was a pioneer in her field. She had an international reputation as an outstanding photographer.

She was born Margaret White in the Bronx in 1904 to a Jewish father & an Irish Catholic mother. She was raised in New Jersey. Her mother instilled in her the drive to strive constantly for self-improvement. She added her mother's maiden name of Bourke to her own when she became an adult.

After graduating from Cornell, she moved to Cleveland. There she started her own commercial photography studio & began to focus on both architectural & industrial photography. An innovator in her own right, she brought along a new style of magnesium flare to a steel plant. This in turn produced white light, which allowed her to capture the making of steel. She gained prominence for doing this. As a result of this she was hired to become an associate editor & staff photographer for the fledgling "Fortune" magazine, a post she held from 1929 till 1935.

Henry Luce was so impressed with her work for "Fortune" that he made her the first female photographer for his new "Life" magazine. Indeed her photograph of the construction of the Fort Peck Dam graced the cover of "Life's" first issue in 1936.

Margaret became the first female war correspondent. She was in the then Soviet Union when Hitler's German troops invaded Russia & she captured many photos of that action. She came close to being wounded or killed on numerous occasions throughout World War II. She was with General George S. Patton when the concentration camp at Buchenwald was liberated.

She both interviewed & photographed Mohandas Ghandi mere hours before his 1948 assassination.

Margaret continued on at "Life" magazine until 1957. She then chose to become a part-time employee there due to the onset of Parkinson's Disease. She fully retired in 1969.

Married twice & divorced, Margaret Bourke-White passed away at Stamford Hospital from Parkinson complications in 1971.

She was 67 years old.

WHO SAYS INDUSTRY ISN'T PICTURESQUE?

(Arthur d'Arazien)

Well, Arthur d'Arazien certainly thought it was.

Arthur took many photos of industrial sites, especially when the rust belt of the north was teeming with heavy industry. Margaret Bourke-White got her start photographing it early in her career. Milton Rogovin took it a step further years later by photographing the workers on the job in the long gone Bethlehem Steel plant in Lackawanna, NY.

But Arthur focused on grand sweeping views of heavy industry facilities. Much of his photographic imagery is captured in a book, "Big Picture: The Artistry of d'Arazien".

He got his start as an assistant to a noted theatrical photographer in New York, who documented Broadway productions. Arthur eventually branched into fashion & commercial photography. He was commissioned by Underwood & Underwood to take pictures of the 1939 New York World's Fair.

His reputation had grown to the point where, during World War II, he taught aerial photography to the U.S. Army Air Corps at Lowry Field in Denver, CO. After the War he began his career as an industrial photographer. It was both his energy & creativity which drew the attention of such various heavy industries as steel, paper, automobile, transportation, & chemistry. They commissioned him to photograph their industrial sites for PR purposes. His photos were such that he was deemed more of an impresario & producer rather than just another photographer. This came naturally to him due not only to his previous work, but to his own skill as as both a painter & a sculpter.

David Haberstich of the National Museum of American History in the Smithsonian Institution had this to say of those industrial photographs: "What Arthur d'Arazien has done is to study his subjects...& convey the truth about their power & impact on the modern era and, in the process, produce exciting, often strangely moving, pictorially fascinating images".

Arthur d'Arazien, a longtime resident of New Canaan, was a founding faculty member of the Famous Photographers School in Westport, CT, in the early 1960's. He passed away at age 90 in Naples, FL, in 2004.

Courtesy of Kent State University Press.

"I THINK YOU'RE GONNA LIKE THIS PICTURE!"

(Syd Greenberg)

So said actor Robert Cummings on his mid-1950's TV sit-com, "The Bob Cummings Show". In this program he was a horny Hollywood photographer of gorgeous models.

But Syd Greenberg was not like that. He took memorable photos of New Canaan & its citizenry. Thus the title.

Syd was a native of New York City, being born there in 1919. He went to work running the darkroom at Weiman & Lester Photoservices & Photorama following his high school education. They had locations in Manhattan as well as Stamford.

He made his mark with his photography during World War II while he served in the US Army Air Corps. His photos of the Chinese theater were well received stateside.

But after the war Syd became attached to New Canaan. He was the official photographer of the New Canaan Police, Fire, & Ambulance departments. He also had photos consistently published in the *New Canaan Advertiser*. He was a very busy man about town with the camera. (Please see his photo on the next page of the carolers on God's Acre on one long ago Christmas Eve.)

Syd Greenberg passed away in 2012 at age 92 as the result of injuries he sustained in an auto accident.

The annual Christmas carol singalong on God's Acre in the mid-1960's.
(Photo by Syd Greenberg in the New Canaan Advertiser.)

"WILL SUCCESS SPOIL MARV THRONEBERRY?"

(Ozzie Sweet)

For those aficionados that couldn't get enough sports when we were kids, we had "Sport" magazine to fall back on. This monthly periodical came loaded with articles similar to the facetious one I wrote about up top. It invariably featured color photos of various athletes as photographed by Ozzie Sweet.

Ozzie was born as Oscar Cowan Corbo in Stamford, CT, in 1918. His mother was a nurse that was an avid photographer. Ozzie got his start as a photographer in the U.S. Army during World War II. At the end of that conflict he had an Army buddy pose as a German soldier surrendering & it made the cover of "Newsweek" magazine.

"Newsweek" hired him as a photographer after the war. Portraiture was Ozzie's forte, as evidenced by pictures he took of a smiling Albert Einstein; Ingrid Bergman clad in a suit of armor for a Broadway play she was in; "Ike" (a.k.a. Dwight D. Eisenhower) as Columbia University's president; & Jimmy Durante with a butterfly perched on his nose. He took such portraits for other periodicals as well, including "Collier's" & "Look". It has been estimated that his photos graced the covers of about 1,800 magazines.

But Ozzie was best known for his portraits of athletes. His 1946 photo of Cleveland Indians pitcher Bob Feller came to the attention of the newly formed "Sport" magazine. They wanted Ozzie to go to work for them, but he protested he was not a sports photographer. The editors of "Sport" told him that's precisely why they wanted his services.

"Sport" came into being a full 8 years before the debut of "Sports Illustrated". Invariably throughout the remainder of the 1940's & both the 1950's & '60's his portraits were on their covers. These included such star athletes as Jim Brown, Joe DiMaggio, Sandy Koufax, Mickey Mantle, Jack Nicklaus, Maurice Richard, & Johnny Unitas.

Ozzie claimed he was highly influenced to do his photos by the paintings of Norman Rockwell. He did photos of children & their pets for other publications. He even shot pictures of pretty girls. He once said of that: "All art editors are fully aware of the pretty girl potential & (they) honestly like to take full advantage of this natural popularity".

Returning to the sports subject, *Sport* magazine readership began ebbing with the advent of the 1970's. McFadden Publications ceased publishing it in the year 2000.

Ozzie Sweet's photos live on in many sports books. He passed away in York Harbor, ME, in 2013 at age 94.

Ozzie Sweet in a "woodie" outside the old Advertiser office on Elm Street.

A TRUE CHAMPION

(Wilky Gilmore)

There was a time, back in the late 1950's, when the New Canaan Rams were state champions in basketball for three consecutive seasons. Much of this success is attributed to Maurice ("Wilky") Gilmore.

Wilky Gilmore, unlike Gary Liberatore (of whom you'll be reading about shortly in his profile), was very tall, standing 6'6". His sister, Marilyn (Gilmore) Washington, said that "he was a perfectionist, but not an individualist. He was a team player".

When Wilky was in 9th grade, that class was still a part of the old Saxe Junior High School further down on South Avenue, opposite the Methodist Church. He was so good at basketball that his 9th grade team beat the NCHS Rams varsity. This certainly brought Wilky to the attention of the late Loren Keyes, who was then the NCHS coach.

Very few Blacks called New Canaan home back then. However, Wilky & his family were not only accepted, but well liked by the community. In fact Wilky was so popular that (at NCHS) he was president of his class for not only his sophomore year, but his junior & senior years as well. He was also a member of Choraleers, played football for the Rams, & served on the student council, among other things.

Wearing basketball jersey # 12 (which is now retired & displayed in a case at the new NCHS), he was a scoring machine. He tallied a record 697 points during the three years he was at NCHS (1955-'58).

"He was like the Pied Piper", said Gary Liberatore. "(He) would come to the elementary schools & talk to the kids & encourage us to study hard so we'd be eligible (to play sports)."

Colleges with strong basketball programs sought out Wilky for their teams. After leading the Rams to three straight state titles, he chose Colorado over UConn because the former was in the "Big Eight". He took them to the championship game one season, but the Colorado Buffaloes lost to Cincinnati.

Wilky was drafted by the NBA's St. Louis Hawks, but a knee injury sustained in college cut short his pro career before it even began. Having a degree in Business from Colorado, he returned to New Canaan & became a CPA. He also went to the UConn Law School & after passing the bar became a partner with Harvey Melzer in a local law firm. He even became a member of New Canaan's first Town Council.

But Wilky wanted to branch out still further. He eventually moved to sunny California & became a sports agent. Wilky's disposition, though, was that of a really nice guy & he seemed out of place in the cutthroat world of sports agents. Nonetheless, he had a sharp eye for young athletic talent. He thought a pair of sisters were going to become stars in the tennis world. They did. Their names were Serena & Venus Williams.

But Wilky suffered from narcolepsy. This contributed to his early passing at age 53 in 1993.

Wilky's remains are interred in Lakeview Cemetery in New Canaan. The caretaker of it, Bo Hickey, said the inscription on his tombstone should read: "Gentleman first....Attorney should be last".

Yes, Wilky Gilmore was indeed a class act!

MAURICE GILMORE

"Skill is the best claim to greatness."

Choraleers 2, 3, 4; Basketball (Varsity
2, 3, 4; All Tournament 2, 3; All County
2, 3; All American 3); Football (Varsity)
2; Golf (Varsity 2, 3); Student Council
(Vice-President 2; Representative 3;
President 4); Math Club 2.

TERRY YIELDS TO ANOTHER TERRY

(Terry Hanratty)

Hey, gang, remember "The Game of the Century"?

That was when the 8-0 Notre Dame Fighting Irish played the 9-0 Michigan State Spartans at mammoth Spartan Stadium in East Lansing, MI, on Saturday, November 19, 1966. Both teams were battling for the top ranking among college football teams. They were both scoring machines, with Notre Dame tallying 301 points in their first 8 games, while Michigan State scored 275 points in its initial nine contests. The frenzied media build up before this game was literally heard around the world. (I know, as I was stationed in South Vietnam when the game was played.)

The final result was a 10-10 tie.

So much for the "Game of the Century".

But Terry Hanratty was hardly at fault. He was knocked out when sacked by Michigan State defensive lineman "Bubba" Smith in the first quarter & was done for the day. (Was "Bubba" a big guy? Well, he stood 6'7" & weighed 280 lbs. One standup comic in a nightclub supposedly said of him when he entered the premises to move to the middle of the cabaret because he was tilting the room.)

Terry was an outstanding quarterback for Notre Dame. He teamed up with wide receiver Jim Seymour for many a score. In his three years on the varsity under head coach Ara Parseghian, Terry completed over 55 % of his passes. He was an 18 year old sophomore for that so-called "Game of the Century". He never won the Heisman Trophy, but was a prime candidate for it from 1966 thru 1968.

Terry was selected in the second round of the annual NFL draft by Pittsburgh Steelers' head coach "Chuck" Noll in 1969. It was Noll's first season in the "Steel City" & Pittsburgh came in dead last in the NFL Century Division, ending up with a pathetic 1-13 ledger. Terry's baptism into the NFL was nothing like what he'd done at Notre Dame. Indeed, he lost the starting QB job to a rookie the following season. His name was Terry Bradshaw.

The Steelers soon climbed into contention as the 1970's moved along. Unfortunately, Terry Hanratty was a back-up QB. He did collect Super Bowl rings for both games IX & X, in which the Steelers downed the Minnesota Vikings by a score of 16-6 in the former & the Dallas Cowboys by a 21-17 tally in the latter. Terry finished his career as a member of the first year expansion team Tampa Bay Buccaneers in 1976. He backed up Steve Spurrier & saw only limited action as the Buccaneers stumbled home with an 0-14 record.

Terry worked as a stock broker for many years after his retirement from the NFL.

That's Terry Hanratty on the left, but who are the other two guys?

BO PLAYS IN THE SNOW

(Bo Hickey)

I first met Bo Hickey at Cherry Street East in New Canaan in May, 2018. The occasion was a "mini-reunion" of New Canaan High School students from back in the mid-1960's. (Needless to say, the lunch & the ambience c'est magnifique!) Bo is the beau of one of my NCHS classmates, Gail (Davidson) Overbeck. Her husband, Don, passed away from cancer many years ago.

Now to me meeting some former professional athlete or other celebrity is no big deal. I once sold replacement windows to former Buffalo Bills' defensive back Booker Edgerson in the "Queen City of the Great Lakes" back in the mid-1970's. When I told my boss about it, he (being the diehard Bills' fan that he was) exclaimed: "You mean THE Booker Edgerson!!?" I thought he was going to have apoplexy when I told him that's who it was.

Yes, Bo did play a season in the old American Football League with the Denver Broncos back in 1967. He shared with me his memories of playing in the snow & ice of the long gone War Memorial Stadium (a.k.a. "The Rockpile") in Buffalo that December. He said it was bitterly cold that day as well. I also didn't envy him for having to shower after the game in the cold water of the old Rockpile.

Bo was a running back who played under former Bills head coach Lou Saban. One of Bo's teammates on the '67 Broncos was the aging "Cookie" Gilchrist, who had been a star halfback for the Bills only a few years before that. But Denver finished in the cellar of the AFL West with a paltry 3-11 ledger in '67. Bo was apparently not included in Saban's plans for the future as he began rebuilding the team, even though he tallied five touchdowns that season. It was assorted injuries that contributed to the brevity of Bo's pro playing career.

The 5'11", 225 pounder had played his college football at Maryland. Prior to that he played at Stamford Catholic High School, where one of his teammates was New Canaan's own Tom Fiore. Tom's dad, Joe, owned the Radio Shop, which graced the SE corner of South & Elm in the late 1950's & the '60's.

Bo got into coaching high school football in both Stamford & New Canaan after he hung up his cleats. True, he does come across as gruff, but there is a kind heart beneath the exterior. Still, you get the feeling you wouldn't want to cross him.

Bo Hickey resides in New Canaan today, where he has gained much respect among the citizenry.

THE CHAMPIONSHIP SEASON

(Gary Liberatore)

The NCHS Rams basketball team was trailing defending Class B state champion Plainville in the waning seconds of the game for all the marbles. But suddenly one of the Plainview players fouled Gary Liberatore. This allowed Gary to get a pair of free throws. He got both of them in the net & ~~~ Voila! ~~~ the Rams were state champs!

All this took place at the Payne Whitney Gym in New Haven on a cold March night in 1962. New Canaanites attending the game went just as wild as the winning players in celebrating the victory! (After all, Plainview was just coming off a 30-game winning streak.)

Redheaded Gary is not a tall fellow, but he was extremely agile when it came to handling a basketball. (His old neighbor Larry Creedon can certainly attest to that!)

Gary Liberatore (pron. "Lib-a-tore") was born in 1944. The family was a fixture in New Canaan, as two of his uncle's had local dining establishments (i.e., Libby's & Paggy's). They were (& are) an energetic family.

Gary lettered in a quartet of sports at NCHS (i.e., football, basketball, baseball, & cross country). He, John Christensen, & the late Don Overbeck were chosen to the All-Tournament Team in '62. Both he & Gorton Wood were named NCHS Male Athletes of the year as well.

Following his 1962 NCHS graduation Gary went to the University of New Haven. He had been awarded a four-year scholarship there for his baseball & basketball skills. He was also selected

First Team All-American ~ All New England there in 1966. Gary remains the all-time collegiate scorer in New England, amassing a record 3,176 points! He was on the varsity team all 4 years at college.

Gary is in the halls of fame for NCHS, Fairfield County, the University of New Haven, & all of New England. He was honored as a gold key recipient by a Connecticut sportswriter, as well as being selected as a basketball All-American in '66 & being named as Outstanding Athlete of '66 by the Knights of Columbus. Gary's jersey number was retired by the University of New Haven.

Gary & I are both Vietnam veterans. He served from 1969 to 1971.

He taught for 43 years as a physical education teacher at the Kit Murphy Elementary School in Stamford, CT. Gary Liberatore is now retired & residing in Naples, FL, with his wife, Carolee.

State Champs!

Varsity Team. First row: Tom Wilhelm, Don Overbeck, Gary Liberatore, Coach Murphy, John Christensen, Gorton Wood, Dick Olson. Second row: Jeff Fuller, Tom Cody, Kevin Sullivan, Dick Zavesky, Jim Saunders, Rit Bickford, Norman Hoffman, Bob Bach.

NOW BATTING FOR THE WHITE SOX, NUMBER 32...

(Ron Northey)

"Rich Stadium in the sa-berbs of Buff-a-lo where this man, numbah 32. O ~~ J ~~" (doggone it, what is his *last* name? I had it right on the tip of my tongue!!!)

Hope you didn't mind my imitation of the late Howard Cosell, gang.

Many famous athletes have worn that number. Ron Northey was not as famous as some of them, but he had a fairly long major league baseball career.

Ron was born in 1920 in Mahanoy City, PA. He was a big man for his height (5'10"). Although most sources claim he weighed 195, he was probably in excess of 200 lbs. His nickname was the "Round Man". He was not known as a fast runner on the base paths or in the outfield.

But Ron could hit. He had 104 RBI's for the wartime Philadelphia Phillies of 1944. He stroked a cool .321 in part-time play for the 1948 edition of the St. Louis Cardinals. But a knee injury he sustained in 1951 kept him out of action for much of the season & his weight ballooned even further. He was sent down to the minor leagues by the Chicago Cubs early in the 1952 season. He languished there until late in the 1955 season when he was purchased by the Chicago White Sox. There he became nearly exclusively a pinch hitter.

He did prove to be a worthy investment for the "ChiSox", as he smacked the ball at a solid .385 clip as a pinch hitter in 1956 (15-for

39). But look at his stats closely. With one exception from 1955 thru his final season in 1957, he only scored runs himself when he homered. Pinch runners were nearly always inserted for him whatever other times he reached base.

I remember Ron from his last 3 seasons. However, his pinch hitting magic seemed to evaporate in 1957 & the White Sox sold Ron to his original MLB team, the Phillies, in late July of that year.

True, he did belt a pinch hit home run in his first at bat for the Phils, which set a then-record for lifetime pinch hit homers. But he batted just .226 that season & called it a career after the season ended. Trivia buffs might take note that he drew a walk from reliever Ed Roebuck in the 9th inning of the September 28th game. It was not only Ron's final major league at bat, but reliever Roebuck was the winning pitcher In an 8-4 Dodger victory; this was played at Connie Mack Stadium (nee Shibe Park) in Philly. This was the next-to-last game of the '57 season & was the final game the BROOKLYN Dodgers ever won.

By then Ron was working in the off-season as vice-president & sales manager of a toy manufacturer in Connecticut, so he had that position waiting for him when he left baseball. He later served as a coach for the Pittsburgh Pirates from 1961 thru 1963 under manager Danny Murtaugh.

Ron Northey passed away suddenly in 1971 just 10 days before his 51st birthday.

(His son, Scott Northey, played briefly as an outfielder for the Kansas City Royals in 1969. He smacked the ball at a .262 pace in 20 games, with one home run & seven RBI's. Not bad stats. I wonder why they didn't bring him back for more action in subsequent seasons.)

"INTERCEPTION!", SEZ SCHENKEL

(Tom Scott)

Undoubtedly CBS play-by-play announcer Chris Schenkel said that on November 12, 1961, when New York Giants linebacker Tom Scott did just that. Tom then ran the ball 65 yards for a touchdown that was frosting on the cake in the Giants' 38-21 triumph over the Philadelphia Eagles at Yankee Stadium that afternoon.

What made it even sweeter for Tom was that he did it against his former team, with whom he made the Pro Bowl twice (1957 & 1958) before being dispatched to the Giants. Tom was a defensive end for Philly from 1953 thru '58 following his college career at Virginia.

But the Giants already had a pair of outstanding defensive ends in Jim Katcavage & Stamford's own Andy Robustelli, so the brain trust decided to place him at linebacker alongside Sam Huff. He came to the NFL's so-called "glamour team", as his timing was most fortuitous.

Tom played on four Giants teams (1959, '61, '62, & '63) that made the annual NFL Championship Game during his half-dozen seasons in the "Big Apple". There were celebrations a-plenty by the Giants, their scribes, & the fans in such watering holes as Mike Manuche's & Toots Shor's following games, which were usually Giants' victories in those days. But the Giants had an Achilles' Heel: they, like the 1990-'93 Buffalo Bills, couldn't win the BIG one. (True, they did beat the Chicago Bears decisively to win the NFL championship in 1956, but they lost that legendary overtime contest to the Baltimore Colts two years later & that's when they hung the albatross around their necks.)

The so-called "glamour team" collapsed in a heap during the 1964 season. The disintegration began when they traded away both Huff & defensive tackle Dick Modzelewski to the Washington Redskins & Cleveland Browns, respectively, following the 1963 campaign. Then age suddenly seemed to hit virtually everyone one else on the roster at the same time & the Giants came in dead last that year with a 2-10-2 ledger. There is a famous photograph of dazed Giants quarterback Y.A. Tittle perched on his knees in the end zone during still another loss late that season. Y.A.'s facial expression seems to echo that song from the musical, "Sweet Charity", which states: "There's Gotta Be Something Better Than This!"

At any rate, Y.A. hung up his cleats at the conclusion of that season. So, too, did Tom.

Tom Scott passed away in Charlottesville, VA, in 2015 just four days before his 85th birthday.

HE WAS DEFINITELY ON THE BALL

(Fay Vincent)

We've had some interesting Baseball Commissioners. It all began in 1920 when the position was established in wake of the infamous "Black Sox" scandal, when eight members of the Chicago White Sox were accused of conspiring to throw the 1919 World Series. The owners decided to hire Judge Kenesaw Mountain Landis, who had a reputation for no nonsense. He ruled the game with an iron hand until his death late in 1944.

His successor was the affable former Governor & Senator from Kentucky, Albert B. ("Happy") Chandler. Whereas Landis was bigoted & refused to let Blacks play professionally except in their own Negro Leagues, Chandler was Commissioner when Jackie Robinson became the first Black player in the Major leagues in the 20th century.

But "Happy" wasn't a pawn for the owners, so in 1951 they selected former sportswriter Ford C. ("It's a League matter") Frick as Chandler's successor. Frick's replacement was retired USAF General William Eckert, who seemed lost in the clouds in that job. Bowie Kuhn, an attorney for the baseball establishment came next, but his personality was boring compared to the NFL's Pete Rozelle. Peter Ueberoth succeeded Kuhn, but the successful businessman didn't last all that long in that position.

Academia was the next choice of the owners & they called on Bart Giamatti from Yale University to be the next Commissioner. Bart was a true baseball fan as well as an intellectual. Alas, his tenure was all too brief, as he suffered a fatal heart attack on September 1, 1989. He was succeeded by his deputy, Fay Vincent.

Fay, too, is a fan of the game. In my opinion he was the game's last good Commissioner.

Fay was born in Waterbury, CT, in 1938. He went to Williams College after graduating from the Hotchkiss School. He had graduated with honors from Williams & thus wound up in the Yale Law School, graduating from the "Old Eli" in 1963. He began his career in a Washington, DC, law firm before going to work for the SEC. He then went on to become the chairman of Columbia Pictures in 1978 & was Executive President of Coca Cola during the 1980's when Giamatti tapped his old friend to become deputy commissioner.

To say that Fay had his hands full in his new position following Giamatti's death is an understatement. For example, the World Series that year was interrupted by a 6.9 earthquake shortly before play was to start at San Francisco's Candlestick Park in the third game of the fall classic. It was a violent 'quake & 31 minutes after it struck Fay (who was in attendance there) ordered the contest postponed.

Play didn't resume again until ten days later due to massive damage inflicted on the Bay Area. The Oakland Athletics completed the four game sweep of the neighboring Giants on October 28th.

The next major crisis came when the owners locked out the players from 1990 spring training. This had to do with the owners proposed salary cap, which the players' union bitterly contested. It took until March 19 to settle matters, as Fay worked with both sides in hammering out some sort of an agreement. The new Basic Agreement raised the minimum rookie salary from $ 68,000 to $ 100,000. Thus the seventh work stoppage came to an end, although spring training was a washout that year. (The MLBPA had their initial strike in 1972.)

Then, in July of that year, came the suspension of New York Yankees owner George Steinbrenner. Seems George had paid some small time gambler to find "dirt" on Yankee outfielder Dave Winfield. This came about after Winfield sued Steinbrenner for allegedly reneging on the $ 300,000 promised for the former's foundation. Fay then suspended George for life, although Steinbrenner was reinstated in 1993, a year after Fay left office.

Fay appointed the Committee for Statistical Accuracy. They ruled in 1991 that Roger Maris was the true single season home run king. Roger had belted 61 home runs in a 162 game season in 1961, but then Commissioner Frick ruled that "Babe" Ruth's record would stand as the mark for the 154 game season, which was how many were played per season prior to '61. (Roger's mark stood until a trio of guys collectively known as "Stevie Steroid" allegedly broke his record in the late 1990's.)

Then there was the Steve Howe incident. Steve was a pitcher for the Yankees in 1992 who apparently was a drug addict. Thus

Fay barred him for life for his repeated failing of drug tests. Upper level Yankee management came to Steve's defense & called Fay's bluff about them also being suspended for life, as they testified on Howe's behalf. This put more pressure on Fay & he resigned the commissionership in September, 1992. (Howe's suspension was subsequently overruled by an arbitrator that November.)

The owners decided to play it safe & appointed fellow owner "Bud" Selig of the Milwaukee Brewers to replace Fay. He said of his three year tenure that "To do the job without angering an owner is impossible. I can't make all 28 of my bosses happy. People have told me I'm the last commissioner. If so, it's a sad thing. I hope (the owners) learn this lesson before too much damage is done".

This author used to be a big baseball fan when he was young, but my interest in the game at the major league level began eroding with the advent of free agency & those atrocious salaries that came about as a direct result of that. In fact, I turned my back on the old National Pastime when both players & owners called off the 1994 World Series. Outside of watching the Chicago Cubs win the 2016 fall classic, I've maintained that vow. To me its no longer a game.

Fay was not afraid to express his opinion on the steroid scandal: "I don't think its an exaggeration to say it's the biggest scandal since the '20's & the Black Sox scandal. The generic problem of steroids in baseball has been brought to a head by the (Barry) Bonds situation. Its really an enormous mess because it has threatened all baseball records, everything that was done in the '90's forward is suspect because of the likelihood that lots of players were using steroids".

Today Fay Vincent maintains a summer residence in New Canaan. He has written several books about baseball.

"THE MORNING MAYOR OF NEW YORK"

(Herb Oscar Anderson)

A friend of mine in Buffalo heard a comedian say this years ago: "Picture Lawrence Welk fronting a Rock group. Mr. Welk might have said something like: 'Okay, boys, let's get-a down, get a funky'".

Herb Oscar Anderson dubbed himself the "Morning Mayor of New York". He also referred to himself as "HOA". (Remember this was LONG before Home Owners Associations.) He seemed to be an anachronism during his heyday on WABC A.M. radio in New York, as he preferred his generation's music to Rock 'n Roll. WABC was one of the top radio stations in the Tri-State area, but one had to listen later on in the day to deejays Charlie Greer, Scott Muni, & "Cousin" Bruce Morrow on that station to get their fill of Rock.

Morning drive time back in the early 1960's was not nearly as progressive as other times of the day. I'm not really sure why that was. Anderson's show was okay, as was fellow New Canaanite Jack Sterling's morning gig on WCBS, but I preferred listening to Ted Brown & the Redhead on WMGM & to low-key radio comedians Bob (Elliott) & Ray (Goulding) when WMGM became WHN.

Mr. Anderson liked to croon. He sang along with his instrumental theme song: "Hello again. Here's my best to you. Are your skies all grey? I hope they're blue!" (He did have a melodic voice.)

Said Dana Webster, who was a classmate of mine at NCHS: "The first thing you noticed about Herb was his size ~~~ well over 6' & 235 lbs., but what you remembered was his voice ~~~ big & booming but full of midwestern openness and a gentlemanly elegance. In all the years I knew him I never saw Herb lose his temper or even his cool.

"I knew Herb more as a neighbor & employer. (As a teenager) I painted his house, mowed his lawn, & babysat his children....(He) left me alone, trusting me to do it right." (One of Herb's kids, John Anderson, changed his name to John James & was a featured player in the old TV series, "Dynasty".)

Herb was indeed a mid-westerner. He was born in May, 1928, in South Beloit, IL. He began his radio career in Janesville, WI, moving to similar gigs in IL, FL, & IA. His big break came with a Top 40 show in St. Paul, MN. He briefly did radio in Chicago before moving on to New York City in 1957. He spent one year with WABC & two more with WMCA before landing the morning drive time show on WABC in 1960.

But the times indeed were changing. Rumor was that Herb became fed up with the direction that Rock music was taking & he quit WABC early in 1969.

Herb often sang along with MOR instrumentals on his WABC show. I remember his putting lyrics to Bert Kaempfert's "That Happy Feeling" & crooning along to it: "When I was a little baby, my mama said to me...."

He did continue on the radio for several more years, his last stint being in Vero Beach, FL.

Herb Oscar Anderson Andersion passed away in Bennington, VT, in February, 2017, at age 88.

(l to r) Jack Sterling, Bob VanDerHeyden, & Herb Oscar Anderson

AN ENGAGING COUPLE

(Mika Brzezinski & Joe Scarborough)

Joe & Mika co-host the a.m. "news" show on MSNBC known as "Morning Joe". I put quotation marks on both ends of the word "news" because their show (just like most of the so-called news shows on MSNBC, CNN, & FOX) is really more opinion than pure journalism. No, I'm certainly not discrediting either of them, as Mika has solid journalistic credentials. Indeed she was at the site of the World Trade Center for CBS when the South Tower collapsed on September 11, 2001.

Mika is the daughter of the late Zbigniew Brzezinski, who served as an advisor to both Presidents Lyndon B. Johnson & Jimmy Carter. She is also the grandniece of former Czechoslovakian President Edvard Benes. Born in 1967, she is a graduate of Williams College in Williamstown, MA.

She functioned as a "news reader" early on in her days with "Morning Joe". She rebelled on the air, refusing to read the report of Paris Hilton's release from jail as the lead story on a June 2007 telecast. She was so incensed by this dictum that she attempted to set that script on fire. Then co-host Willie Geist prevented her from doing that. But Mika had a genuine point to her argument, which I do agree with. She again protested an innocuous story about Lindsay Lohan three years later.

Apparently Joe was quite enamored of her spunkiness, for not only did she become co-host of "Morning Joe", but the two of them fell in love with each other. (By the time your read this they may well have tied the knot. They were engaged as of this writing.)

Joe Scarborough was born in Atlanta in 1963. He received his BA from Alabama & his law degree from the University of Florida.

He was initially elected to congress during the Republican wave of 1994. He was the first Republican to represent Florida's 1st congressional district since Reconstruction. He easily won reelection three more times.

Joe was a conservative congressman. He opposed abortion & voted for Newt Gingrich's proposal early in 1995 that comedian Jay Leno on the "Tonight Show" jokingly referred to as the "Contract ON America". He was opposed to U.S. membership in the United Nations & wanted to make Public Broadcasting self-sufficient. But he was also viewed as a moderate when it came to both the environment & human rights.

Joe then went into television. He eventually replaced Don Imus as the morning host on MSNBC.

Both Joe & Mika were highly critical of both candidates in the 2016 Presidential election. Their feud with Donald Trump is well documented & there's no need to go into that here. As a result of this Joe now considers himself an Independent. I do agree that much of what is discussed on their show is to protect the Constitution.

Have I been opinionated in this portion of the book? To some degree.

These are indeed trying times. Many of us of both stripes (liberal & conservative) long for the days of good objective journalism from the likes of Walter Cronkite, as well as Huntley – Brinkley. We fondly remember the days when we all liked "Ike". Dwight D. Eisenhower was indeed a very good (& IMO) MODERATE

President. The country was at peace for nearly all of his presidency & was prosperous as well. Congressmen & Senators certainly compromised back then, with few exceptions (the junior Senator from Wisconsin, Joseph R. McCarthy, comes to mind).

Most of us agree (at least in our age bracket) that we are indeed being bombarded with "news" on a 24 hour basis. We abhor some of the more extreme ones of both stripes that scream at each other: "I'm right!"; "No, I'm right!" Its not just the commentators, but our elected officials in Washington as well.

As for the citizenry, don't go voting for politicians just because they wave the flag & go to church on Sunday. Stop acting like sheep.

There are some people who think that Fascism can't happen here.

Think about all this, folks.

With that, I rest my case.

Pere

(J. Burgi Contner)

I know some sons attempt to follow their fathers in the same profession, with varying results. In the case of the Contner's, both were quite successful.

J. Burgi Contner was a noted cinematographer. He was born in Peoria, IL, in 1906, but grew up primarily in Lakeland, FL. He got a job as a projectionist at the local movie theater at the age of eleven. This opened up a whole new world of possibilities for young Burgi. One of the initial things he did was take these silent films to the local VA hospital so wounded servicemen could view them. For those unable to sit up, he screened the movies on the ceiling.

Burgi (pron "Bur-Gee") was a tinkerer who had a seemingly endless curiosity about motion picture equipment. Among the things he invented were a two-color film process & an early sound system, among other things. Technicolor became the industry standard several years later, as it is a three-color process, but Burgi was a pioneer of early motion picture color. He also invented (according to son James) "a device that went into the projector's aperture (which) created a uniform format on the movie screen. Until this time there was no standard format". Burgi was but 23 years old when he did this. It became the film industry standard for the next 20 years; it also became the same when television came along.

He married a woman named Betty Harris in 1941 in Miami. He had filmed the waterskiing & hydroplanes at Cypress Gardens in Florida, but they soon moved to New York. There Burgi opened a motion picture equipment rental business, although he always owned his own equipment. He designed & built a 35mm camera, the Cineflex, for use in combat by the US Armed Services.

He had filmed several low budget movies, but he climbed on board the burgeoning TV industry in the late 1940's. Since most of these shows were done in New York, he didn't have to travel far at all to work. By 1951 he was successful enough to move to New Canaan. At first he & his wife rented, but a year later they purchased the sprawling home of Stanton Griffis, who had served as US Ambassador to Poland, Egypt, Argentina, & Spain. One of the first things Burgi did at their new house was convert the huge dining room (35' long x 20' high) into a movie theater. This featured two interlocking 35mm projectors in a soundproof booth on the second floor, as well as an electric curtain. (This house was on Smith Ridge Lane, off Route 123.)

Apparently Burgi didn't mind the early morning commute to New York, as his workday began at 7 a.m. Among the series he was the director of photography on were "Car 54, Where Are You?" "The Defenders", "The Goldbergs", "Naked City", & "You Are There". Cast members & directors were invited to the Contner abode for soirees that son James described as "quite popular & notorious".

Burgi & Betty became very involved with the Town Players (see COMMUNITY LEADERS) during the 1950's & '60's. Young Jim later on joined them in it. They became friends with Paul Killiam.

Burgi converted the basement of their home into a machine shop, ably assisted by Ray Fairty, a local machinist. Burgi became enamored of the new stereophonic sound. He built theater stereo amplification equipment in that basement. Eventually he had to hire more help for it as it became a tremendous success. (As the song sez from the 1957 movie musical, "Silk Stockings": "You got to have glorious technicolor, breathtaking cinemascope, & Stereophonic Sound". ~~~ Words & music by Cole Porter, BTW.)

In 1967, after 50 years in the film industry, Burgi felt it was time to call it a day. He & Betty retired initially to the Bahamas, but then relocated to Miami in 1972.

J. Burgi Contner passed away in Coral Gables, FL, in 1973 at age 67.

ET FILS

(James Contner)

One of the reasons I never got into the world of big business was the rat race of it. I'd seen the toll it took on many such men.

Thankfully, New Canaan exposed me to far more culture than I would have gotten in most locales, which is why I gravitated toward the arts. James Contner, I'm sure, feels likewise.

Jim Contner was born in New York in 1947. Jim attended New Canaan public schools except for one year at Lenox Prep School in

Massachusetts, after which he returned to NCHS. He enjoyed playing football, soccer, & tennis.

But he got involved with Town Players as a kid, landing a role
in Paul Killiam's original production of "Next to Heaven". Paul's son,
Tim, was a classmate of Jim's & were in that musical together. Jim
also learned about dancing through Mrs Johnson's Dance School &
Walter Schalk's School of Dance. (See COMMUNITY LEADERS
for the latter.)

He worked as a delivery boy for the Main Market. He dated
Jayne Tippman at NCHS. Her father was Walter Tippman, who
is profiled under COMMUNITY LEADERS. Eventually Jim &
Jayne tied the knot.

Jim was uncertain just what he wanted to do following high
school graduation. He thought about taking a year off before going
to college, but then he & an NCHS classmate, the late Mike Devlin,
decided to go to Miami-Dade Junior College. They became room-
mates & helped support themselves by painting apartments in
their complex.

But Jim & Jayne really loved each other at the time. They wed
in August, 1967, & moved back to Miami. They settled into the
Coconut Grove section of Miami, which at that time was a hub for
artists & hippies. He went on to the University of Miami while Jayne
found modeling assignments. Jayne, a pretty blonde girl, had a story
similar to actress Lana Turner, in the fact that she was discovered by
a New York fashion photographer at the Elmcrest Luncheonette.
She was 16 at the time & thus began her modeling career.

Jim had wanted to get into the film school at the U of Miami,
but there was a long waiting list, so he became an English major
instead. Upon graduation he & Jayne moved back to New Canaan

& rented a house on Marvin Ridge Road. He decided to emulate his father & join the film industry.

He had to climb the ladder slowly, as does most everyone else. He became second assistant cameraman on such films as "Rivals" & "Born to Win". It was on the latter that he hooked up with Jack Priestley, who was a camera operator when Jim's dad worked on the TV series "Naked City". Priestley hired him as first assistant on second camera on second unit for the Oscar winning 1972 film, "The Godfather". Afterward, while working on the film, "Across 110th Street", Jayne became pregnant. Their first child, daughter Elisha, was born in January, 1973. They were now able to buy a small house across from the Silvermine Tavern in Norwalk.

Gordon Willis, the primary cinematographer on "The Godfather", called Jim & asked him to be first assistant on second camera for the sequel to that film. He accepted & it changed his life, as it put him in a higher echelon of assistant cameramen on the east coast. He had worked with camera operator Ralph Gerling on "The Way We Were". Ralph was unable to do the next project for director Steven Spielberg, but he recommended Jim for it. The film was "Jaws".

Jim & Jayne were now able to buy a larger house, which was the old Silvermine Forge. It needed lots of renovation. Jayne was left to cook on a hot plate & microwave while Jim was off shooting "Jaws". The eight week shoot turned into five months of filming on Martrha's Vineyard.

His first primary operating job was on the TV series, "Movin' On", which starred Claude Akins & Frank Converse about a pair of 18 wheeler drivers & their varied adventures. Jim soon filmed such movies as "Superman: The Movie" (1977), "The Wiz", "All That

Jazz", & "On Golden Pond", among others. (It was during "Movin' On" that their second daughter, Megan, was born, in October, 1975. Their son, Nicholas, was born on New Year's Day of 1979.)

More film & TV work came Jim's way, but in 1985 Jim was hired to replace the cinematographer on the TV series, "Miami Vice", midway through the show's first season. Since this was one of the most popular shows of the 1980's, Jim & Jayne decided to sell their CT home & relocate to Boca Raton, FL. But Jim ended up quitting "Miami Vice" six episodes into its second season, due to personality conflicts. So he returned to doing feature films. This necessitated extensive travel. This was compounded even further by his work in Chicago directing the TV series "Crime Story". It began putting a serious strain on their marriage.

Jim enjoyed directing TV shows, even though they necessitated lengthy hours. He wound up directing episodes of "The Equalizer", "21 Jump Street", & "Wise Guy". But all this success unfortunately led to the dissolution of Jayne & Jim's marriage, according to Jim.

Eventually he met producer Penny Adams on the TV series "Midnight Caller". They wed in 1994. Jim soon hooked up with writer & producer Josh Whedon, who produced both the TV series "Angel" & "Buffy, the Vampire Slayer". He ended up directing nearly all the episodes of those two shows. (Jim said this was so lucrative that "it paid for a lot of colleges".)

But by the turn of the last century the directing assignments had pretty much dried up. Jim came to the realization that "this business is a young man's game". Penny is three years younger than Jim, but she decided to exit show biz when he did. They moved to Richmond, VA, to be closer to both family & grandchildren.

Yet Jim was not completely finished with it all. The local film community in Richmond called him to work as a cameraman on local films. This led to a four-year teaching gig for both Jim & Penny in the Cinema Program of Virginia Commonwealth University.

These days Jim & Penny Contner are enjoying both traveling & retirement.

HE'S WITH "THAT GIRL"

(Phil Donahue & Marlo Thomas)

Yes, Phil Donahue is definitely with the star of that former ABC-TV prime hit of the abovementioned title.

Most of you know him as the longtime host of "Donahue". Phil was an innovator in having his studio audience actively participate in his show. He had a 29 year gig in that capacity, focusing on controversial issues that divided liberals & conservatives on his long running syndicated show. (It ran from 1967 till 1996.)

Phil's show started out in Dayton, OH. He relocated it to Chicago in 1974, then moved it to New York City 10 years later. No other syndicated talk show has had such a lengthy run.

Back in the 1980's Phil, being raised a Catholic in his native Cleveland where he was born in 1935, broke the story of the molestation of children by Catholic priests. Many strongly objected to that story when he introduced that topic, but history has since vindicated Phil.

He hosted another show on MSNBC, starting in June, 2002. But he was vocal in his opposition to the war in Iraq & executives at that network canceled his show the following February.

––––––––––––––

His wife, Marlo Thomas, is the daughter of comedian Danny Thomas. She was born in Detroit in 1937. She is of Lebanese & Italian descent.

Marlo guested on many TV shows from 1960 through 1965, including "The Many Lives of Dobie Gillis", "77 Sunset Strip", "Thriller", "Bonanza", "McHale's Navy", & "Ben Casey". Then came her major breakthrough.

In 1966 she came up with her own idea for a sitcom. It concerns a young woman who decides to leave home in the upper reaches of Westchester County & become an actress in New York City. The stories revolved around her struggling to make good as an actress, working at various temp jobs while making the rounds of auditions. Her boyfriend was portrayed by actor Ted Bessell. The show was a hit & lasted until 1971.

Both ABC & Clairol executives (the latter being her principal sponsor) wanted her to end the show's run with she & her boyfriend tying the knot. But Marlo refused that idea, feeling that it sent the wrong message to her mostly female audience in the early days of Womens' Liberation.

After "That Girl" left the air, Marlo did a pair of specials entitled "Free to Be...You and Me".

In addition to work in both Broadway & Off-Broadway shows, as well as films, Marlo guest starred on such TV shows as "Roseanne", "Friends", "Ally McBeal", & "Law and Order SVU".

FAME CAN BE FLEETING

(Faye Emerson)

How many of you over the age of 65 are familiar with that name? Yet, in the early 1950's, she was known as the "First Lady of Television".

Faye was born in Louisiana in 1917. She moved with her mother to San Diego as a child. Not long before World War II she decided to become an actress & soon moved to Los Angeles. She became a starlet & acted opposite such leading men as Zachary Scott, John Garfield, & Van Johnson. "The Mask of Dimitrios" (1944) opposite Scott was probably her most notable film.

She made the jump to network TV in the early days of it, acting in such anthology series as "The Philco Television Playhouse" & "Goodyear Television Playhouse". She guested on variety shows as well. Such exposure came to the interest of network honchos & she was given her own TV program, "The Faye Emerson Show", in 1950. CBS built a studio for her program on the 6th floor of the Stork Club Building, which was a replica of that society night spot's famed Cub Room. She also created quite the controversy in those conformist days by wearing low cut dresses & blouses, thereby showing the top part of her ample breasts.

That program only lasted for a year, but she came back with an ambitious & expensive show titled "Faye Emerson's Wonderful Town", which was telecast live from June of 1951 till April of the following year. One may be thinking this program had only to do with New York City. Au contrare, dear reader. The show traveled to different cities & town, broadcasting live from Boston; Louisville; Minneapolis; the Bronx; Los Angeles; Hanover, NH; & San Diego, among many other locales. But the cost of doing such a show led to its demise. That, plus it was on opposite "Your Show of Shows" on rival NBC, which starred Sid Caesar & Imogene Coca. (It aired on Saturday nights at 9 pm eastern time.)

Faye hosted a couple of other TV shows for the next few years, including one co-hosted with her third husband, bandleader "Skitch" Henderson. Eventually the title "First Lady of Television" went to Lucille Ball.

Faye stayed active on TV through the remainder of the '50's, but only by serving as a panelist on such game shows as "I've Got a Secret" & "To Tell the Truth". She always made a fashion statement by showing up dressed in elaborate evening gowns. But after her 1957 divorce from Henderson she virtually disappeared from the small screen.

In all Faye was married 3 times. Her first husband was a Naval aviator by whom she had her only child, a son. She married Elliott Roosevelt (the son of Franklin D. & Eleanor) in 1944 while FDR was still President. (They divorced in 1950 & she quickly wed Henderson.)

Faye Emerson lived the remainder of her life as a recluse. She passed away in 1983 in Majorca from stomach cancer.

INFORMATION, SIL VOUS PLAIT

(Clifton Fadiman)

Clifton Fadiman wore many hats during his 95 years here on earth. He was certainly an intellectual, but he also was an author, editor, & both radio & TV personality.

The squire of Richards Lane was born & raised in Brooklyn. He became a Phi Beta Kappa graduate of Columbia University. Following graduation he taught English at the Ethical Culture High School in the Bronx, but he soon landed a job at Simon & Schuster. When he interviewed with Max Schuster, Clifton pulled out a folder in which he had 100 ideas for books, including putting Robert Ripley's "Believe It or Not" into book form. Once hired he translated the German children's tale, "Bambi", into English for publication here.

Clifton continued expanding his horizons. He remained at Simon & Schuster when he became the editor of the "New Yorker" magazine's book review, a position he held from 1933 to 1943.

In 1938 he began hosting the popular network radio show, "Information Please!", which he did until 1948. The regular panelists were Franklin P. Adams, John Kieran, & Oscar Levant. They had a guest expert from one field or another every week. When author John Gunther guested, Clifton asked him about Iran, by wittily asking: "Are you shah?", to which Gunther replied, ""Sultanly". (This quote was obtained from Wikipedia, BTW.)

Television beckoned in 1949 & Clifton hosted "This is Show Business" from 1949 till 1954. This program featured musical entertainment combined with the performers airing their problems with the show's panelists. These panelists included Abe Burrows, George S. Kaufman, & Sam Levenson. Playwright Kaufman created the biggest brouhaha during the show's run in December, 1952, when he attacked the commercialization of Christmas by stating on the air: "Let's make this one program on which no one sings 'Silent Night'". Viewers got so irate that Kaufman was temporarily banned from the show.

Clifton was quite the sage, saying on one occasion: "When you reread a classic, you do not see more in the book than you did before. You see more in you than there was before". Another time he said this of a writer: "He has no grace, little charm, less humor...(and) is not really a good storyteller".

He fit right in with such TV intellectuals of the 1950's as Bennett Cerf, John Charles Daly, the aforementioned George S. Kaufman, & Alexander King.

Clifton Fadiman was twice married, producing one son by his first wife & both a son & a daughter with his second. He passed away from pancreatic cancer in Florida in June, 1999.

That's Clifton Fadiman seated on the left, next to Sam Levenson.
This was the set of "This is Show Business".

"AND NOW WE HAVE OUR LITTLE FRIEND…"

(Jim Fowler)

I can still remember the late Marlin Perkins using phrases such as that on the old TV show, "Mutual of Omaha's Wild Kingdom". (That phrase is describing a small animal & NOT Jim Fowler!)

Jim was Marlin's co-host on that program. The series first aired on NBC in January, 1963. It remained on that network until 1971 when it went into syndication. Most of the shows after '71 were repeats, although new programs were occasionally produced until 1987.

Perkins was the primary studio host, with Jim out in the field. Comedians such as Johnny Carson lampooned that show, imitating Perkins saying something such as: "I'll wait someplace safe while Jim is doing (whatever with some dangerous animal)".

Mutual of Omaha was the sole sponsor of that program, when it was becoming extremely rare to be a sole sponsor as the 1960's progressed. But "Wild Kingdom" opened up new avenues to the viewing public about both environmental & ecological perception. That show also was filmed in very exotic locations such as Africa & along the Amazon River in South America.

But "Wild Kingdom" was not without controversy. The CBC TV network in Canada did an investigation, which resulted in a televised report entitled "Cruel Camera". The CBC news magazine program "Fifth Estate" claimed that "Wild Kingdom" staged scenes & were cruel to animals. They cited an example by saying that the capture of a bear in the swamps of Florida was purportedly a bear the show had already placed there. Perkins denied these allegations on camera.

Jim took over as host when Perkins retired in 1985. Marlin passed away three years later. Jim retired in 2000 at age 68. But Jim was certainly active on NBC, making many appearances on "The

Tonight Show" when the aforementioned Carson hosted it. He served as the official wildlife correspondent on "The Today Show" for many years.

In 2002 the Animal Planet began broadcasting new "Wild Kingdom" specials, once again sponsored by Mutual of Omaha (albeit sans Jim).

I do like the following quote of Jim Fowler's: "The continued existence of wildlife & wilderness is important to the quality of life of humans. Our challenge for the future is that we realize we are very much a part of the earth's ecosystem, and we must learn to respect & live according to the basic biological laws of nature".

HE WASN'T SILENT IN NEW CANAAN

(Paul Killiam)

Paul Killiam was known nationally for programs he did on TV re: silent movies.

When he produced & narrated "Silents Please" on ABC back in 1961, he was initially quite caustic in his narrations. But he began to realize that many silent films were quite good & needed to be preserved. Thus he proceeded to do so for most of the remainder of his life.

Silent movies have been satirized in the past. The 1952 MGM musical "Singin' in the Rain" accurately described the transition from silent films to "talkies" in the late 1920's. Sound indeed did ruin several careers. When I taught the 1920's in my U.S. History course at Tonawanda (NY) Senior High School, I used to speak in a very high pitched voice & tell my "good & faithful students" about how some handsome leading men were traipsing the streets of Hollywood back then, saying "Why won't they hire me anymore? I'm a matinee idol!"

Paul got so serious about preserving silent movies (most of which were filmed on nitrate) that he loaned part of his silent film collection to a series broadcast on PBS in 1971. Orson Welles was recruited to host this series which presented a dozen silent film classics, such as "The Gold Rush" (with Charlie Chaplin); "The Son of the Sheik" (Rudolph Valentino); D.W. Griffith's "Intolerance"; "The General" (Buster Keaton); & "The Thief of Bagdad" (Douglas Fairbanks), among others. The program, "The Silent Years", was well received & helped open the eyes of the public to these virtually neglected treasures of yore.

But what of Paul Killiam himself?

He was born in 1916 & went to college at Harvard. His parents wanted him to be a lawyer & he did go to law school at Boston University. But he had trod the boards as a kid & said of his experience: "There's just nothing like the feeling of getting applause. Whatever is the ham in me, drives me....(T)he reward....is being in a show yourself". He both directed & performed in the Hasty Pudding shows at Harvard & also wrote for the *Harvard Lampoon* during his undergrad years in Cambridge.

He got a job performing in the Max Liebman production, "New Faces of 1937". He toured with the show throughout New England before it landed on Broadway, where the show's title was changed to "Who's Who".

He paid his way afterward through law school employed as a radio announcer. Following graduation he got a job as the news & special events supervisor at radio station WOR in New York.

After World War II he & two friends discovered an old movie house that was for rent on 2nd Avenue. The trio leased it & turned it into a cabaret modeled on the Old American Music Hall, which had been a New York institution. People began calling this place "The Old Knick". The entertainment was old-fashioned, consisting of silly puns, audience sing-alongs, & old melodramas where one could "hiss the villain". Then unknown actors & actresses just starting out were hired to perform there. Gene Barry was the house villain & Cloris Leachman was the young ingenue in distress. Jack Lemmon waited tables in the audience. (His son, Tom, told me that Paul used to screen old silent movies between acts at the "Old Knick".)

But times (& tastes) change. The Old Knick was a victim of that, closing its doors in 1953. He moved to New Canaan as the decade moved along.

He joined Town Players & directed their production of "The Pajama Game" in 1958. But he was frustrated with how the show turned out, so he switched gears & wrote original material for TP to perform. The first one was a send-up of New Canaan life & the commuters therein, with the title "My Fare, Lady". One of the songs sounds straight out of Allan Sherman: "The brains urbane ride mainly on the train", but it was all Paul.

He scored a big hit with "Next to Heaven", which TP did in late 1960. He skewered much about New Canaan life in it, with one memorable scene in which an 1880's businessman spoke of the glories of commuting between New York & New Canaan, telling the audience how it takes just over an hour to ride home to Connecticut on the train. "Just think how fast everyone will get home to New Canaan in 75 years!" (This drew a huge laugh from the audience, as folks of that time knew of the many delays on what they referred to as the "New York, New Haven & Hardly Able Railroad"!)

Next came "The Fireman's Flame", memorable for the silent film comic melodrama that Paul shot on the old Lapham estate (now Waveny Park, for those of you taking notes). That came along in 1961.

The creative & witty Paul began writing Christmas carols for commuters in 1962. One of them, "The 12 Days of Commuting", took to task "rest rooms overflowing, air hose not a-hosing, wires down at Rye, fire at Cos Cob," etc.

Such original work continued through the years. He used to emcee local Gridiron Club roasts of prominent local people. But he kept writing his own productions for Town Players.

In 1983 he did a history of New Canaan titled "To Thee We Sing". Two of the stars were Joan Brainerd & James Noland, both of whom I knew as soloists at the Congregational Church when I was at NCHS years before. He satirized an old 1830's law that forbade parishioners from selling alcohol except for medicinal purposes. Paul, serving as narrator, quipped to the audience: "This didn't decrease the number that got drunk. It increased the number who got sick".

Paul said of his local productions: "When one sees guys like Jack Lemmon going on to world fame, you do wonder, 'Could I have done it?' But I'm inclined to say, 'No, it wasn't for me...I'm not eating my heart out. Obviously I get some satisfaction out of the shows we do here. And I must be giving the people something they enjoy, because they keep coming back to see my next one.... It's just that, in my spare time I don't play golf or go to Las Vegas. I do this".

He resided in New Canaan for many years, raising four children. He passed away in Norwalk in 1996.

Yes, Paul Killiam was indeed quite a guy!

ABOUT THAT WATER CLOSET

(Jack Paar)

Hey, gang, here's a trivia question for you: Who preceded Johnny Carson as host of the "Tonight Show"?

'twas Jack Paar.

One can say that Jack immediately followed Steve Allen, who was the original host of the "Tonight Show", but you'd be wrong. (More later.)

You younger readers may well ask who was Jack Paar anyway?

Well, he was "kinda/sorta" a jack of all trades. He was a movie actor, radio & TV comedian, a talk-show host, & an author. Jack was born in 1918 in Canton, OH, but his family moved to Jackson, MI (south of Lansing) when he was a child. He overcame a stuttering problem as a youth.

He got his start on radio in Jackson, then got announcing jobs in Detroit, Indianapolis, & Cleveland before coming to WBEN radio in Buffalo in the early 1940's. Following military service during World War II, Jack began ascending the network radio ladder. He pinch hit as host of "The Breakfast Club" & served as a panelist on "The $ 64 Question". Jack Benny thought enough of Paar's talent to have him serve as his summer replacement in 1947.

Jack performed in a few movies as well, portraying Marilyn Monroe's boyfriend in the film, "Love Nest" (1951), among other roles. He hosted radio's "$ 64 Question" in 1950, but he began getting a reputation as a spoiled kid in his battles with network honchos. He also performed as a stand-up comic on the "Ed Sullivan Show" in the early '50's.

All this exposure led to TV gigs for Jack. He hosted a pair of game shows ("Up to Paar" & "Bank on the Stars". CBS decided he would be perfect as the host of "The Morning Show" as 1954 began & he did those short lived honors. Unfortunately, NBC's "Today" show kept clobbering "The Morning Show" in the ratings. After that Jack did guest appearances & guest hosting on other TV programs.

Well, Jack's life would change for the better as 1957 went along. But first a bit of background on the show he was to inherit.

NBC Programming Director Sylvester ("Pat") Weaver noted the success of the "Today" show & he decided to put on a late night variety show in the fall of 1953. It was decided to just air it locally on the NBC TV affiliate in New York, but Steve Allen made the program such a rousing success that NBC gave "The Tonight Show" a full network offering in the fall of 1954. Allen was so well loved by the network brass that they also gave him a Sunday night prime time show in the summer of 1956. That, too, was a big success.

But therein lay a problem. Allen really tired of the duties of doing both shows, so NBC hired comedian Ernie Kovacs to host "The Tonight Show" two nights a week. Still, the daily grind of it all was wearing on Steve, so he quit "Tonight" in January of 1957. Kovacs decided to exit the show at the same time.

So what to do about the the late night slot?

Well, some genius at NBC came up with the idea of having the show completely revamped so it would be just like the "Today" show. Jack Lescoulie & Al ("Jazzbo") Collins were recruited to do the hosting honors on "Tonight: America After Dark". Unfortunately, the show went dark 6 months into its run. Both viewers & critics thought it was ill conceived.

The network brass thought about bringing back a variety-like format & decided to take a chance on Jack Paar. He accepted the duties & began hosting "Tonight" that July.

Fastidious character actor Franklin Pangborn was the original announcer on that show for Jack, but network honchos didn't think he was enthusiastic enough. So he was jettisoned in favor of Hugh Downs. (Paar's old Army buddy, Jose Melis, led the musical combo.)

Whereas Allen was quite uninhibited on his "Tonight" show, Jack opted for a different approach. He had a bunch of guests show up regularly on his show, including Cliff Arquette (in character as Charley Weaver), Peggy Cass, Zsa Zsa Gabor, French comedienne Genevieve, Dody Goodman, Alexander King, & Tedi Thurman

("she being "Miss Monitor", the sultry weather girl on that NBC network radio show back then. ~~~ Remember the old "Monitor" beacon, gang?)

Jack had some good writers on his staff. These included Dick Cavett & Jack Douglas, the latter being a one-time resident of New Canaan.

Jack also thrived on controversy. He went to Cuba in 1959 to interview the new leader there, Fidel Castro. He openly feuded with syndicated columnists Dorothy Kilgallen & Walter Winchell. Through all this he had his loyal viewers.

Paar also battled NBC over censorship. One night in February, 1960, he became quite volatile. This had to do with the network eliminating a supposedly controversial joke about a European water closet from the taped broadcast. The following night he abruptly walked off the show in protest, leaving a stunned Hugh Downs to complete that night's hosting duties.

As for the joke itself, judge for yourself whether or not it should have been censored:

"An English lady is visiting Switzerland. She asks about the location of the W.C. The Swiss gast haus clerk, thinking she is referring to the Wayside Chapel, leaves her a note that read: 'The W.C. is situated 9 miles from the room you will occupy....It is capable of holding about 220 people & is open only on Sunday & Thursday... It may interest you to know that my daughter was married in the W.C. & it was there she met her husband...I shall be delighted to reserve the best seat for you, if you wish, where you can be seen by everyone.'"

Jack's temper tantrum certainly led the newspapers for the next 3 weeks, as he stayed away from his show for that long. He finally returned to the airwaves on March 7 by telling both the studio audience & viewers: "As I was saying before I was interrupted..." This drew loud cheers from those assembled in studio 6B at 30 Rock. He went on to say: "I believe my last words were that there must be a better way of making a living. Well, I've looked... & there isn't". This drew huge laughter from those assembled there.

But Jack in that same monologue got frank & stated: "Leaving the show was a childish & emotional thing. I have been guilty of such action in the past & will perhaps be again. I'm totally unable to hide what I feel. It is not an asset in show business, but I shall do the best I can to amuse & entertain you & let other people speak freely, as I have in the past".

Jack eventually tired of the daily grind & quit the show for good in March of 1962. He was replaced by Johnny Carson at the beginning of October that year, with rotating hosts filling in during the transition period.

Jack was still under contract to NBC, however, & he wound up hosting a prime time show, "The Jack Paar Program", on Friday nights. On this show he travelled to Africa to interview Dr. Albert Schweitzer & also showed film clips of the Beatles a month before their U.S. debut on the "Ed Sullivan Show". On another program he had the recently defeated California gubernatorial candidate play the piano. That was Richard Nixon.

Paar's Friday night effort lasted from 1962 to 1965. After that his TV appearances were few & far between, which was mostly his choice.

Jack Paar died in Greenwich, CT, in January, 2004.

PEACE THROUGH DIPLOMACY

(Raymond F. Burghardt)

I first knew Ray Burghardt when we were 6th graders at the Congregational Church in New Canaan. No, this wasn't Sunday school. Rather it was when they decided to put 6th graders into Saxe Junior High School, due to the rapidly growing population. A new high school was being built at South Avenue & Farm Road, but it wouldn't be completed until mid-way thru the 1956-'57 school year. Thus, half of the 6th grade was dispatched to the Congregational Church, while the other 50 % went to St. Aloysius. We moved into the old high school (which became the Saxe Annex) early in '57. (For those of you taking notes, we had Mr. Howell Rice as our 6th grade teacher.)

Ray was born in New York City in 1945. His family moved after Ray's sophomore year at NCHS to Morris County, NJ. His parents felt the school system there was mediocre in comparison to New Canaan's, so Ray graduated from the private Blair Academy in western New Jersey in 1963.

He went to Columbia, majoring in Political Science & graduating in 1967. He then went on to Columbia's School of International & Public Affairs (SIPA) for one year. He passed both the written & oral exams for the U.S. Foreign Service, but was told by the examiner afterward that there were currently NO openings in that field then due to a hiring freeze. But the examiner urged Ray to join the Peace Corps, which he did.

Once in the Peace Corps, Ray was sent to Colombia. His fiance, Susan Day, accompanied him to that South American country.. She taught at an American school there, but Ray jokes that she came along so he wouldn't be tempted by Colombian girls.

After only one year in Colombia, Ray was informed that a diplomatic post had opened up for him ~~~ in South Vietnam. He wasn't all that thrilled about going there initially, but accepted the post anyway. He & Susan decided to get married prior to "deploying" over there, which they did in Cape Cod. (Ray & Susan were in South Vietnam from October, 1970, thru April, 1973.)

Once in 'Nam, Ray became part of a provincial advisory team, which he did for the first seven months he was "in country". True, this involved some travel from Saigon "out in the field". Ray realized there was possible danger & encountered some of it, but overall called that experience exhilarating. (Being a Vietnam combat veteran prior to that, I referred to that experience with adjectives NOT fit for publication here.)

Susan, meanwhile, managed the "GI Call Home Service" at the USO in Saigon. She also raised their new daughter, who was born six months before they left Vietnam.

After those seven months were up, Ray moved to the American Embassy. There he became the "go to" guy on religious matters with the local Catholics, Buddhists, & other religions in country. These religious groups functioned as political parties in the dysfunctional government of South Vietnam.

In all Ray & Susan spent 22 years in Asia. He was a China Watcher based in Hong Kong from 1977-1980. Later on came Beijing from 1987 through 1989, initially as a political counsellor, but serving as Deputy Chief of Mission during his final months there. Sadly, he viewed the infamous massacre of demonstrators by Chinese government forces in Tiananmen Square from a U.S. Embassy room in the Peking Hotel.

He was dispatched to Seoul, South Korea, as the Deputy Chief of Mission from 1990-'93, serving as Acting Ambassador (or Charge d'Affaire) during his last 6 months there. The Clinton Administration appointed him as Deputy Ambassador to Manila (1993-'96); Consul General in Shanghai (1997-'99); & to a full ambassador-rank position in Taiwan (1999-2001). Ray did point out that Taiwan does not have an American Embassy anymore, as its referred to as the "American Institute in Taiwan". Ray went there when the newly elected Taiwanese government (in Ray's words) "took a hostile view toward Beijing, causing fear in Washington of tension that could draw us into a conflict. Dealing patiently with the new (Taiwanese) president & calming the situation was one of the high points of my diplomatic career".

Ray had diplomatic postings in this hemisphere as well, serving in Guatemala (1973-'75) & Honduras (1982-'84). He is fluent in Spanish, Chinese, Mandarin, & Vietnamese.

He served on the White House National Security Council staff from 1984 till 1987, reporting to President Ronald Reagan on Latin American affairs. He accompanied then Vice President George H.W. Bush on seven trips to Latin America, referring to the Greenwich (CT) native as "one of the finest people I've ever met".

What goes around comes around, as Ray closed out his formal diplomatic career as U.S. Ambassador to Vietnam from 2001 through 2004, to which he was appointed by President George W. Bush. After his retirement from the State Department in '04, Ray & Susan moved to Honolulu. There he went to work for the East-West Center, which he describes as a "wonderful educational &

research organization dedicated to collaboration between Asians & Americans to improve relations & to solve issues together".

Ray Burghardt is primarily retired now, but still does pro bono work for the East-West Center in an advisory capacity, as well as offering advice to other Asian concerns.

CALL HIM MR. AMBASSADOR

(Paul W. Speltz)

Paul Speltz has had quite the career for himself in the world of international finance and government service. His Asian experience has been quite unlike mine.

Ambassador Paul W. Speltz is the Chairman, Founder, and CEO of Global Strategic Associates, LLC (GSA). For over 40 years, Paul has lived and worked in Asian business and finance, both in the private and public sectors.

Immediately before launching GSA, Paul served as President of Kissinger Associates, Inc. for several years. Prior to that, he was nominated by President George W. Bush to serve as the U.S. Ambassador to and Executive Director of the Asian Development Bank (ADB) in Manila. In this role, Paul represented the United States extensively throughout Northern, Southern, and Central Asia to expand regional trade, promote financial cooperation, and increase private sector lending and financial activity. In 2004 United States Secretary of the Treasury John W. Snow concurrently designated Paul the Financial and Economic Emissary to the People's Republic of China, in which capacity Paul spearheaded the U.S. government's economic and financial cooperative initiatives with China.

Prior to serving as Ambassador, Paul spent 20 years as a prominent member of the international business community. He served as Managing Director of Global Operations for New York-based Bluestone Capital and as a Senior Director and Advisor on Asian geopolitical activities for United Technologies Corporation (UTC). In 1972, Paul started his own business in China and Asia, which over the years first merged with ATC International and, in 1981, he sold this firm to Citicorp. Following the sale, Paul stayed with Citicorp in China and Asia as a Vice President Citicorp.

Paul is a member of the Bretton Woods Committee and the Board of Directors of the Pacific Pension & Investment Institute. Paul also serves on the International Advisory Board to President Jin Liqun of the Asian Infrastructure Investment Bank (AIIB). Paul is a member of the Council on Foreign Relations, the Council of American Ambassadors, the Asia Society, the U.S.-China Business Council, and the National Committee on United States-China Relations.

Paul is a 1965 graduate of New Canaan High School and he earned both his Bachelors & Masters degrees at UConn. He resides with his family in NYC and New Hampshire.

Yes, he has been (& is) a very busy individual.

That's Paul W. Speltz on the right; his brother David is on the left.

MAN'S INHUMANITY TO MAN

(Ralph K. Andrist)

New Canaan High School had some truly excellent social studies teachers when I was a student there in the early 1960's. One of them was Robert Reed (profiled earlier under "Educators").

Though he taught Modern History my sophomore year, he nevertheless informed his class about how cruel we were to the Native Americans (at that time referred to as Indians). This came about when we talked about early European explorers & settlers. He then went on to elaborate how we American white men broke virtually every treaty with them through the years.

Back in the movie & TV westerns of the mid-20th century, the Indian was the "bad guy". Somehow the U.S. Cavalry always came to the rescue of those menaced by these "savage red men" just in the nick of time. (Not sure just how the Cavalry did so, considering that there were no cell phones back in the day.) But this was a sorely distorted view of the American Indian, Historian Ralph K. Andrist set out to set the record straight.

Ralph wrote a book titled "The Long Death: The Last Days of the Plains Indians" in 1964. He focused on our treatment of them from approximately 1840 onward, although he did go into some detail about the forced removal of the Cherokee tribe from Georgia & South Carolina when Andrew Jackson was President back in the 1830's. (I did a term paper on it while at Buff State & compared it to the infamous Bataan Death March during World War II.)

Ralph pulled no punches in his tome. He wrote about the good, the bad, & the ugly incidents & people involved back in the 19th century. It is not meant to horrify, but to clarify. His book was well received.

Ralph was born in Minnesota & graduated magna cum laude with a degree in Journalism from that state's University in 1937. This being the Great Depression, he worked as a gravedigger, carpenter, & freelance publicist before serving in the U.S. Navy during WWII.

He became a radio station news editor in Minneapolis after the war. Some of the documentaries he worked on won awards. He later served as a garden editor for "Better Homes & Gardens" in Des Moines, Iowa, prior to moving to New Canaan, where in New York City he served as a publicist for the Crusade for Freedom & raised funds for the Episcopal Church Foundation. He did freelance writing on the side.

The American Heritage Publishing Company hired him as a book editor in 1964. He served in that capacity until 1970. He was senior editor of the Franklin Library, a division of the Franklin Mint, when he retired in 1979.

He wrote other books as well, which focused on the Erie Canal, the 1849 California gold rush, & the Lewis & Clark Expedition, among other topics.

Ralph Andrist had three daughters during his 41 years of marriage. He passed away at age 90 in 2004.

"FALLING IN LOVE WITH LOVE"

(Helen Fisher, PhD)

Thankfully, Dr. Helen Fisher does NOT think of the above title in the negative connotation that Lorenz Hart did when he penned this back in the 1930's. Rather, she has made a very thorough study of the subject of love over the years.

Helen is the twin sister of Lorna VanParys-Fisher (previously profiled under ARTISTS). Both ladies grew up in a glass house on Ponus Ridge, which Helen thought was "a huge amount of fun". (Although my Uncle Art, after whom I was named, did warn me one time that: "People who live in glass houses shouldn't *take baths*".)

Though she went away to Shipley, a private boarding school in Bryn Mawr, PA, after her freshman year at NCHS, her heart remained with New Canaan. She graduated Shipley in 1963 & then went for a dual major in both Anthropology & Psychology at NYU. Helen earned her Doctorate in 1975 at the University of Colorado. She wrote in her doctoral thesis "on the evolution of human female sexuality & human pair bonding". In this dissertation she "addressed the question ~~~ why do humans form pair-bonds to rear our young, while some 97 % of other mammals do not. Love is a hallmark of our species".

Helen has "conducted extensive research & written 6 internationally-selling books on the evolution & future of human sex, love, marriage, & gender differences in the brain". She also developed "the first personality questionnaire based on neurobiology & validated with fMRI brain scanning", which has now been "taken by 14 (+) million people in 40 countries. I wanted to understand what people mean when they say: 'We have chemistry'. Indeed, with this research, I feel I have snuck into Mother Nature's kitchen & finally see how your natural personality style shapes who you are & who you love".

Helen is "currently a Senior Research Fellow at the Kinsey Institute of Indiana University & Chief Science Advisor to the internet dating site *Match.com*". Among the half-dozen books she has authored are: "Anatomy of Love"; "Why Him?, Why Her?"; & "Why We Love".

She has "traveled to 107 countries on short junkets...Most exotic were North Korea, Tibet, New Guinea, Mongolia, the Trobriand Islands, Tajikstan, Surinam, & Ethiopia. All were fascinating ~~~ & everywhere people loved". Helen also believes that "love is an evergreen topic. Around the world men, women (and children) pine for.., live for..., kill for,..& die for love ~~~ and my anthropological perspective lends some scientific insight."

Helen feels that she was "always an anthropologist. As a child, I would sneak into the woods behind our house, sit on an old stone wall, & watch our neighbors eat dinner in their glass house. But I began to study romantic love earnestly in grad school. My interest started in a psych class where I was being taught that all behavior was learned. As a twin, I didn't believe it. So I began to reason that if there was *any* aspect of human behavior that must have evolved, it would have been our reproductive strategies. Hence my studies of romantic love, attachment, and the other *inherited* emotions & motivations that evolved to find & keep life's greatest prize: a mating partner".

She gives a lot of speeches these days, including at both the U.N. & the G-20 and is a five time TED All-Star. She also does many T.V., radio, & print interviews.

Helen Fisher resides in Manhattan. She finds New York City "enormously exciting".

As to her own love life: "Well, no one gets out of love alive. We all suffer...I'm with a magnificent man today....(I)f I die tomorrow, I will regard my life as incredibly lucky. Lucky to have grown up in New Canaan, ...to have lived a life devoid of war on my doorstep,... to be in good health,...& incredibly lucky to have had the opportunities that have miraculously come my way".

SOME PEOPLE NEVER SEEM TO AGE

(Lynne Hugo)

When my NCHS graduating class held their 50th reunion in October, 2013, some of the attendees marveled at how a trio of our classmates looked. The threesome (Russ Nebbia, Russell Struck, & Claire Watson) looked as if they had just stepped out of the pages of our senior yearbook.

The same can be said of Lynne Hugo, who graduated there two years after I did. She still looks like the same cute girl I knew in Mrs. Sasanoff's Dramatics Club.

There has always been a certain freshness about Lynne, much like a gentle summer breeze. She is the author of a dozen books. While most are fiction, she has also published a volume of creative non-fiction, as well as a children's book & two books of poetry.

Lynne's family moved to New Canaan from neighboring Darien just before she began second grade at South School. Her parents were from Holyoke, MA, & had suffered (as had countless others) through the Great Depression. They were determined to become members of the upper middle class.

Lynne, like many of us, didn't truly appreciate all the educational advantages we had in New Canaan until she left there. She loves music & still remembers being awakened to it at Saxe Junior High, by songs she can still sing, such as "Give Me Your Tired, Your Poor", which Irving Berlin had adapted as a song from the Emma Lazarus poem for his Broadway show, "Miss Liberty". She felt likewise about Mrs. Jane Hilton when she joined Choraleers as a freshman at NCHS. Mrs. Hilton also gave Lynne piano lessons.

In addition to Choraleers, Lynne was with *The Spectator* & the aforementioned Dramatics Club. Other teachers who were influential to her were Matt Coyle & Warren Allen Smith of the English department, as well as Dr. James Kerley & Blaine Leighton, both of whom taught Social Studies.

Following NCHS she had a dual major in English & Psychology at Connecticut College. She fell in love while there & married her husband, Alan de Courcy, in the college chapel. She taught English in Chicago for three years while she worked on her Masters in Psychology at Miami of Ohio. She got a position as Clinical Director of a treatment facility afterward. When a crucial funding levy failed, she went into private practice. She was with a five physician medical practice for 21 years.

While her children were still growing she began writing again. Among her books are: "The Testament of Harold's Wife"; "A Matter of Mercy"; "Remember My Beauties"; "Swimming Lessons"; "Graceland"; & "When the Trail Grows Faint". (The last named tome concerns a year in the life of a therapy dog team.)

Lynne says she "writes in black Wal-Mart capri sweatpants. They don't start out as capris, but I routinely shrink them in the dryer by accident. And I always buy black because it doesn't show where I've wiped the chocolate off my hands".

She also said that she loses herself "in crafting language by a window with bird feeders hanging in the branches of a Chinese elm (tree) towering over the house. When I come up for air, I hike by the ponds & along the river in a nearby forest with my beloved Lab. My husband, with whom I planted that elm as a sapling, joins us when he can".

Today Lynne Hugo & Alan retain their residence in Ohio. She sez her Labrador literally emulates "Snoopy" by playing shortstop with a tennis ball.

WHAT? NO TRIBBLES?

(Preston Neal Jones)

The curtain had just closed after the junior class production of "The Madwoman of Chaillot" at NCHS on March 16, 1962. I was literally stunned & stood transfixed for a moment after that, which is when a young guy stormed in from stage left, as if he'd just witnessed his team winning the seventh game of the World Series.

"You were great!" he said as he vigorously pumped my hand. "You were as good as (John) Carradine was in that role!"

I quickly came back to reality & quipped: "Preston, you were only a year old when Carradine was in that on Broadway!"

Yes, that was Preston Neal Jones who said that to me. Preston & I knew each other from when I was introduced to him in Dramatics Club mere weeks earlier. We've been friends for many years now.

Preston graduated NCHS in 1965. He went on to earn his Bachelors of Fine Arts degree at Carnegie Mellon University in Pittsburgh. There he studied acting, directing and writing. Of these three crafts, he has devoted most of his attention to writing.

His initial foray into cinematic oral history came with the article, "James Whale Remembered," as published in the magazine, *Famous Monsters of Filmland*. Whale directed such horror films as the original "Frankenstein" (with Boris Karloff), "The Old Dark House," "The Invisible Man" and "Bride of Frankenstein." (Whale also directed the 1936 film, "Show Boat", which featured many members of the original 1927 Broadway cast. To me it's far better than the glossy, yet empty, 1951 MGM version of it. But that's another story.)

Preston's first book was "Heaven and Hell to Play With ~ The Filming of 'The Night of the Hunter", which was a terrifying 1955 film about a psychotic religious zealot who terrorizes some children in order to find the money their late father had stolen years before. Robert Mitchum did an excellent job as that "whacko" & Lillian Gish was outstanding as the matron who comes to protect the kids. "Hunter" was the first – and, as it turns out, the only – movie directed by actor Charles Laughton. Initially a box office failure, Laughton's film is now regarded as a masterpiece of American cinema. Preston's book on "The Night of the Hunter," based on his interviews with cast and crew, won a "Rondo" Award as Book of the Year from the Classic Horror Film Board.

Preston's other writings have appeared in such publications as *Cinefantastique* & *American Art Review*. He is very active in both the TV & film industry, having served in such varied capacities as creative advertising executive, script analyst, & production assistant. (His very first professional film job was as a p.a. on "The Swimmer," starring Burt Lancaster, which was shot in New Canaan and all over Fairfield County in the summer of 1966.) He has introduced film screenings of "The Swimmer," "The Night of the Hunter," and other films at American Cinematheque & the Los Angeles Film School.

When it comes to music, he's been active there as well. He has contributed entries to "Groves' New Dictionary of Music and Musicians," as well as "The St. James Encyclopedia of Popular Culture." He has also written liner notes for modern day recordings of such Golden Age composers as Alfred Newman, Frank Skinner and Hans J. Salter, among others. He has lectured on the topic of film music at UCLA.

He was also writer in residence at Roanoke College in Virginia. There he taught on such subjects as "The Night of the Hunter," "Star Trek," and American History.

Speaking of "Star Trek", a more recent book he penned was "Return to Tomorrow," which traces the old TV series' resurrection into "Star Trek - The Motion Picture."

Preston Neal Jones resides in Los Angeles, where he has recently completed writing his first work of fiction, an Arabian Nights fairy tale novel for young readers, "The Orphan of Basrah."

Photo by Nancy O. Rich.

A WALK WITH THE SPIRIT

(John Mogabgab)

"Have you been to any of your class reunions?", asked John Mogabgab on the phone with me one night. I was recently divorced & residing in Buffalo, NY, at that time.

When I told him I hadn't, he urged me to attend one. "It's amazing how everything has changed! The old cliques are gone & everybody enjoyed just being with each other!".

John graduated NCHS in 1964. He was a very intelligent student & served as the valedictorian at his graduation. His parents were from Cyprus. They were realtors in town.

I had some church business to do with John, as I was a long time Deacon in First Presbyterian Church in Buffalo. He was one of the editors of the daily devotional guide, *The Upper Room*. I've subscribed to that since the early 1980's, but that one day in the mid-1990's my curiosity was aroused. Was this indeed the same guy I knew years before in New Canaan? I left a message on his work voicemail & he returned my call that evening.

We had quite a chat for maybe 15 minutes or so. He told me about how his parents had been on the cruise ship, the *Achille Lauro*, when it was hijacked by the PLO in 1985. Thankfully, they were unharmed.

John & I had hoped to get together one day. He talked about me coming to Tennessee, which was where he lived then. We never got together in person, but I cherish the memory of that phone conversation.

John was born in New York City on Christmas Eve in 1946. He went to Bowdoin College in Maine, as did one of his NCHS classmates, Jonathan ("Jot") Ross. John was consistently on the Dean's List & graduated cum laude. He was awarded a Rockefeller Brothers Theological Fellowship as a senior there.

He next went to Union Theological Seminary in New York, where he earned a Masters Degree in Divinity in 1972. Then it was off to Yale University, where he garnered a Master of Philosophy in 1975 & his Doctorate in 1978. He met Marjorie Thompson at the Yale Divinity School & they wed on August 8, 1981.

Marjorie had been a Research Fellow with Henri Nouwen. John & Henri hit it off, as the former became a teaching & research assistant to the latter. They formed a life-long friendship as a result of this. John edited several of the books that Henri wrote.

Elaine Eskesen, an NCHS classmate of mine, lost her mother many years ago. She was only 59 when she passed away.

John came to the Manning house (friends of Elaine) in New Canaan to celebrate her mother's life. The two were old friends. John waved across the crowded room to her, but no words were exchanged between them. Instead John mailed her a package containing a book, "Letter of Consolation" by the aforementioned Henri Nouwen. John knew that Elaine was also going through a stressful divorce at the time of her mother's death which is why he did this. He went a step further & invited her to come to Yale Divinity School to personally meet Henri.

Elaine & Henri also became good friends. They found solace in their mutual grief, as Henri's mother had also recently passed away. She stated that what both John & Henri did "brought me back to a spiritual connection I had left behind many years earlier".

John & Marjorie lived for a time in Stamford, CT, where she became Associate Pastor of the First Presbyterian Church in that city. That is the modern designed church that is shaped like a fish. Some in my confirmation class at the Congregational Church in New Canaan referred to it as the "Holy Mackerel".

John, in the meantime, was leading spiritual retreats for the Episcopal Diocese of Connecticut. He also was on the advisory group from which emerged the Academy for Spiritual Formation. This Academy remains an integral part of *The Upper Room* ministries. John became the Theologian in Residence with the Academy.

John soon joined the staff of *The Upper Room* in 1985. He became the founding editor of *Weavings*, which is a spiritual journal of the Christian life. He shepherded that publication for the next 25 years. He also served as an editor on books published by *The Upper Room*. He took a position on the Henri Nouwen Society board following Henri's 1996 passing. This soon merged into a partnership with *The Upper Room*.

Sadly, John passed away on August 8, 2014, the 33rd anniversary of his marriage to Marjorie. They resided in a suburb of Nashville then.

Did John literally "walk the walk"? Consider this quote from from a man named Bradley Delaney shortly after John's passing: "I am proud to say that I was John's roommate for a year while he was a student at Union (Theological Seminary) & I was at Columbia. John was one of the kindest & gentlest men I've ever known. I still remember (him) venturing into sections of the Bronx where not even police or firemen would venture...in order to give some spiritual hope to the people who were squatting there."

"PEYTON PLACE" REVISITED?

(Rick Moody)

Back in the mid-1950's a New Hampshire woman named Grace Metalious wrote a thinly veiled book about her hometown. It became a best seller due to, well, all sorts of moral failings on the parts of the characters in her tome. The name of it was "Peyton Place".

Along came Rick Moody & he more or less did the same thing in his 1994 novel, "The Ice Storm". His book primarily focused on a pair of dysfunctional families in New Canaan during a Thanksgiving weekend in the early 1970's. The book was highly praised by critics & Moody gained a measure of fame, so much so that a movie was produced (& partially filmed in New Canaan) by the same name.

In all fairness to Rick, I have not read that book. I don't know how faithful the film is to the book. But I have seen the movie. Talk about a "downer"! New Canaan is given an unflattering look there. (Now, remember, this is all my opinion.) Ang Lee directed that 1997 film, which featured such noteworthy actors & actresses as Tobey Maguire, Kevin Kline, Joan Allen, Sigourney Weaver, Christina Ricci, Elijah Wood, & Allison Janney.

As for Moody, he was born in New York City in October of 1961 & grew up in both Darien & New Canaan, among other suburban locales. He is a graduate of Brown University. He socked it to the northern New Jersey suburbs in his first book, "Garden State" (1992). Novels after "The Ice Storm" include "Purple America", "The Diviners", "The Four Fingers of Death", & "Hotels of North America". He currently teaches at NYU, according to Wikipedia.

There was one teenage boy in the film, "The Ice Storm", that reminded me of a kid I knew back around the time Moody was a baby. This was the kid who flew his model airplanes filled with lit firecrackers so they would explode. The real life kid was a freshman when I was a junior at NCHS. One afternoon our PE class was canceled. This freshman kid decided to flush a lit center fuse down a toilet in the boys' locker room. Thus, gym was canceled that day due to flooding.

Well, I've given my opinion on Rick Moody's "The Ice Storm". Again, in fairness to him, I will say that the film version is a matter of taste. It just isn't mine.

HEALING THYSELF

(Janet Richmond)

Janet was born in Connecticut. Tragically her parents were killed in an auto accident when she was just 18 months old, an only child. She was very fortunate to have an aunt & uncle that took her in and raised her as one of their own. As a result, her cousins became her sisters.

Even while growing up in a loving home, Janet had emotional difficulties early on in her life. She was too young to understand the premature death of her parents. Instead she was left with the emotional experience of the two most important people in her world just disappearing one day. That left a major imprint on her life moving her into a world of fear, confusion, and a complete lack of worth, a childhood with recurring nightmares, numbness, and putting up a front that all was normal. She was (to quote Langston Hughes) "laughing on the outside, but crying on the inside".

Despite chronic anxiety much of her early life, Janet was very grateful for the education she received in New Canaan, as well as the numerous friendships she developed along the way. With the rampant shyness she lived with, her close friends were her lifeline.

Janet first attended the Country Day School before entering the public schools in 3rd grade. She continued on in NCPS through 9th grade (Center School, Saxe and then one year in NCHS), when (like her adopted sisters) following a family tradition, she went to a private boarding school, the Masters School in Dobbs Ferry, NY. This prep school was a tough one, Janet said, demanding academic & cultural excellence, but in hindsight, it was clear that the work done there prepared her well for UNC at Chapel Hill where she earned her BA.

At UNC, Janet became fascinated with Anthropology. She found here like thinking. Janet observed growing up was that often people were judged for being different, even if different meant the weird car they drove or the 'wrong' kind of plants around someone's house. Small things maybe but for Janet, the judgments made her feel uncomfortable. Anthropology is a science based on the idea that beliefs and behaviors are often the result of the societies & cultures we grow up in. There were no judgments that some behaviors/peoples are bad and some are good. The foundation of this approach validated for her the idea to respect and accept differences between us, that we are all people bottom line and that inclusion rather than exclusion was the way to go.

Janet was also at UNC during the height of protests against the Vietnam War. Still very shy, she did not get into the alternative lifestyles of "free love" & the drug scene. But she now feels strongly that such protesting has led to more equality for all, though of course there is more work to be done.

Following graduation, Janet worked for the Save the Children Federation in Tucson, AZ, working primarily with the Papago and Yaqui Indians. This enabled her to take more of the "the veils & blinders off" and to grasp an even bigger picture of the world & the people in it. Eventually, she moved back east to Manhattan. She taught at a private school in there for 3 & ½ years. While she loved the school and her job, she also suffered from chronic anxiety and depression, to the point where she began to see why some people kill themselves.

The breakthrough came (though Janet didn't realize it at the time) when a friend of hers in NYC suggested that she relocate to Los Angeles. Janet had never been there, but at some level it just felt right. She moved there in 1977 & within three days she fell in love with it. First up was earning her Masters at the UCLA Business School of Management. Still the anxieties & self-doubts persisted.

What changed Janet's life, about 4 or 5 years later, was a conversation she had with her hairdresser. He told her about a psychic named Joan Culpepper and handed her a cassette tape recording of his own reading. Blown away by it, Janet went to see Joan and never looked back. The reading included tarot cards and something called a "Higher Selves soul scan". Joan explained to her that the Higher Selves were more highly evolved soul aspects from the 5th Dimension & from whom she obtained higher-level information.

Although Janet didn't fully grasp everything at the time, the Higher Selves gave her the extraordinarily broad overview of her soul's journey over eons of time ~~~ her evolutionary mission for billions of years! And as if that weren't enough, they also gave her a simple technique on how to release the anxiety. With nothing to lose she tried it. The chronic anxiety was gone within days. From that point on Janet attended many classes & workshops that Joan offered to learn more. Four years later Joan moved out of the state, but Janet continued to work with the Higher Selves on her own & developed her own skills.

In her everyday life, Janet started and ran her own bookkeeping and business management company from her own home for 20 years while raising two wonderful children as a single parent. The whole family thrived beautifully. Her son is now lives in West Los Angeles and her daughter in Houston, TX.

Sadly, 23 years after their initial and continual contact, Joan Culpepper died suddenly in 2006. Fortunately, the connection had been a deep one because Joan's daughter gave Janet the copyright to all Joan's material. Over the next three years, while having the almost 1000 of Joan's cassette tapes (with the Higher Selves information) transcribed onto the computer and preparing for the sale of her management company, she wrote her first book, *"CHOICES: Neutralizing your Negative Thoughts and Emotional Blueprints"*.

In 2009, Janet began her present career, not only preserving the legacy of Joan Culpepper, but paying forward all the help Janet had received. Janet has conducted many workshops, meetup groups and has made numerous TV appearances. She also has her own weekly web-radio show called the Higher Self Voice. Her second book, *"Soul Psychology: Our Journey Through the Human Kingdom Universe"*, published in 2016, won a gold medal in the category "NEW AGE: Mind, Body, & Soul". Janet has also developed her own ability to heal, doing her own powerful version of healing Soul Scans in the many private sessions and radio shows she has done for almost 10 years.

Janet indicates that by using the techniques she learned, her life has turned around so much that grief, fear, shame, lack of self-worth, etc. (toxins of the mind so to speak), have disappeared. She has also expanded her physical health to the point where her doctors make comments – all good - as her blood pressure and cholesterol levels are low, there are no chronic conditions and her body weight is balanced.

Today, Janet is working on her third book: *"Jane & Company: The Unsung Heroes"*, hopefully out by early 2020. Janet resides in the San Fernando Valley in the Los Angeles area.

"I HAVE HERE IN MY HAND A LIST...."

(Allan Sloane)

Say, gang, if you were a kid in the 1950's, it was a fun time to be growing up. We let our imaginations run loose when we played cowboys & Indians; we loved such new toys as Mr. Potato Head, the Hula Hoop, & the Slinky; TV was new & a feast for our eyes & ears.

If you were an adult back then, you loved the booming economy & you also enjoyed TV as much as your kids did. But there was also the paranoia of the Cold War.

A demagogue named Joseph R. McCarthy set the standard for running roughshod over people suspected of having communist ties. Many people were blacklisted, particularly in show business & the media.

One victim of this was Allan Sloane.

Allan was a writer initially for print, but graduated to radio & TV scripts. He was born in New York City in 1914, but raised in New Jersey. After college he wrote for the *Cape Cod Colonial*, *Parade*, & the *Philadelphia Bulletin*. He served in the US armed forces during World War II.. He won a Peabody for his writing of "The Man Behind the Gun", which dealt with the 1943 allied invasion of Sicily.

After the war he began writing radio scripts. He penned them for United Nations Radio & the United Jewish Appeal. However, in 1952 he was blacklisted by CBS & his career as a scriptwriter appeared to be at an end.

Allen persevered, though. Using a pseudonym, he wrote many episodes of such TV shows as "Navy Log" & "Hawk" (the latter starring a young Burt Reynolds). As the 1950's progressed, he wrote TV scripts of 1 & ½ hours duration. He had an emotionally disturbed child & wrote an episode, "And James Was a Very Small Snail" for the TV program "Breaking Point". For that 1963 show he was nominated for an Emmy, as he also was for his script of "Teacher, Teacher", which was aired on the "Hallmark Hall of Fame" in 1969.

He finally garnered an Emmy for "To All My Friends on Shore" in 1972, which dealt with Sickle Cell Anemia. This starred Bill Cosby and it was filmed entirely in Norwalk. Allan's son, Jonathan, relates that Cosby played penny ante poker one night with his parents. Apparently Jonathan's mother took Cosby to the cleaners in that card game.

Allan Sloane passed away in April, 2001, at age 86.

KEEPING THE PROPER PERSPECTIVE

(Pamela Curtis Swallow)

"You've got to Accentuate the Positive,

Eliminate the negative,

And latch on to the affirmative.

Don't mess with Mister In-Between."

(The above lyrics are from the 1944 song hit, "Accentuate the Positive". Music by Harold Arlen & lyrics by Johnny Mercer.)

Those lyrics played a pivotal role for Pam Swallow as life went on for her.

Pam has a buoyant personality. She has had that as long as I've known her, & that goes back as far as 7th grade at Saxe Junior High.

Her parents were both teachers at the private Country Day School in New Canaan. Both she & her older brother Bill were students there. Their mom & dad were very involved in the life of the Congregational Church, as were both Bill & Pam.

Pam was in my graduating class ('63) at NCHS. She became an English major at Skidmore College afterward. She married an actor while attending there. As he was not in college then, he was drafted. Thankfully, he didn't go to Vietnam. Instead they assigned him to duty in Colorado. Pam decided to transfer to college at the University of Colorado. (She sat next to future ice skating Olympic champion Peggy Fleming in one of her classes there.)

Making their home in a cottage in Colorado Springs proved fortuitous for Pam, as the Colorado School for the Deaf & Blind was located right across the street from them. Pam got a job as a gym teacher there. She said she "even taught the students, both male & female, how to waltz!"

Pam actually went to her third undergraduate school when she & her husband returned east, completing her BS at NYU. She then earned her Masters in Library Science at Rutgers. She worked with children in the elementary school grades & she sez she truly enjoyed it!.

The kids loved how she read to them. Informed that she's a natural storyteller, she was inspired to write children's books. The real "young 'un's" enjoy her "Groundhog Gets a Day", while the middle elementary grades like her "Melvil & Dewey" series.. The older elementary grades prefer such titles of Pam's as "Wading Through Peanut Butter", "Leave It to Christy"; & "It Only Looks Easy". (Her book titled "No Promises" is for older kids.)

But Pam was hit hard with a cancer diagnosis as time went on. It apparently was quite advanced when doctors diagnosed it.

I'm going to to get personal here & talk about the cancer the VA Hospital found in me early in 2016. Agent Orange in Vietnam was the culprit in my case, as I was diagnosed with lung & lymphatic cancer. Surgery was necessitated for removal of part of my right lung; I took 8 hits of chemo for the latter. Thankfully, they caught my cancer late in stage one & I'm still in remission as of this writing.

Many of the members of my class were there with love & support, as were friends both here in Charleston & in Buffalo. Facebook friends & my family were very supportive as well. Jim Sanders of NCHS '63 & Bill Englehardt of '66 told me they are cancer survivors, as did others. But no one was more inspirational to me than Pam.

She beat Stage 4 cancer!

Doctors told her that her days were numbered, but Pam took on an attitude of gratitude as well as an outlook that could well have been adopted from the lyrics of the Arlen-Mercer song. She sez of that experience that she has "always been determined. I stuck to my guns & soldiered on. I created marching songs when I took my daily walks in the fields & I hugged the huge tree where my second husband & I tied the knot. To the bewilderment of all the doctors, I beat the odds".

This was over 15 years ago. Pam felt well enough to serve on our eleven person committee that planned the 50th reunion of NCHS '63. (I did not know of her battle with cancer until I was diagnosed with my own 3 years later.)

Pam wrote "The Life and Remarkable Career of Ellen Swallow Richards" in 2014. Her ancestor lived from 1842 to 1911. She was not only the first female admitted to the Massachusetts Institute of Technology, but she was the first woman to teach there as well!

Pam Swallow resides today in the middle part of New Jersey.

"THE NEXT STATION STOP
IS WESTPORT"

(Sloan Wilson)

Say, gang, how many of you back in the 1950's had dads that wore gray flannel suits & commuted weekdays into Grand Central Terminal? These were the businessmen of their day. William H. Whyte wrote a best selling book entitled "The Organization Man" in the middle of that decade which dealt with corporation CEO's insisting on conformity.

Nearly simultaneously with Whyte's tome came Sloan Wilson's "The Man in the Gray Flannel Suit". Both books criticized corporate thinking in those supposedly halcyon days.

Sloan's book dealt with Tom & Betty Rath, a fictional couple in one of the bedroom suburbs of Connecticut. He was a (hopefully) rising young executive in New York. Both felt trapped in the suburban lifestyle & the resultant conformity in both their lives. The late David Halberstam in his book, "The Fifties", quoted Sloan as writing: "Without talking about it much they both began to think of the house as a trap, and they no more enjoyed refurbishing it than a prisoner would delight in shining up the bars of his cell".

Sloan Wilson was born in Norwalk, CT, but grew up in both Florida & the Adirondack Mountains of New York state. He graduated Harvard in 1942 & subsequently became an officer in the U.S. Coast Guard. He commanded a naval trawler for the Greenland Patrol & an Army supply ship in the Pacific.

But with World War II over, he went to work as a reporter on the "Providence Journal". He loved writing & was happy doing what he did. However, the pay was paltry & he & his wife had two children at that time. (A third child, their son, came along later.)

"What we all talked about in those days was selling out", Sloan later wrote. "Selling out was doing something you did not want to do for a good deal more money than you got for doing what you loved to do."

Sloan worked as a writer for Time-Life after the war, but he felt stifled. He was now a man wearing a gray flannel suit, commuting into "The City" from New Canaan (where he lived from 1947 till 1951, according to his daughter, Lisa). True, he did get promoted at Time-Life. Nevertheless he felt he was in a "rat race". He loathed his lifestyle & work, especially after all the excitement & responsibility he had during the War.

Gregory Peck & Jennifer Jones starred in the 1956 movie version of "The Man in the Gray Flannel Suit". It is worth watching. In all Sloan wrote 15 books, including "A Summer Place", which was made into a movie in 1960. He also wrote his autobiography, "What Shall We Wear to This Party?", in 1976.

Sloan suffered from alcoholism his entire adult life. He & his first wife divorced. His wife Elise moved she & their two daughters back to New Canaan while Sloan resided in New York City. But Lisa has said that he remained a loving father who was there to support them, despite his battle with the bottle.

He married for the second time in 1962. He died in 2003 in Virginia at age 83.

AFTERWORD

Well, gang, there you have it.

I hope you enjoyed this book.

I certainly do encourage any of you readers to do your own such book. I did mine for the same reason I helped organized the 50th reunion of NCHS '63: the fact that we're not getting any younger & a sincere wish to remember the days of our youth.

The New Canaan of my youth has long vanished. The fields we used to romp in back in elementary school are where Fieldcrest Road, Farm Road, & Tommy's Lane are now located. (My dog Salty killed a few muskrats over there & deposited them on our front lawn, proud of his trophies.) Ditto the fields now occupied by Saxe Junior High & the YMCA. The woods encompassing the old Lapham Estate are mostly gone. (We ignored the "No Trespassing" signs & went in there anyway back in the day.)

Here's a head start for anyone wishing to take this on. Bob VanDerHeyden has a very interesting career in radio; Margaret Nagel is a well known screenwriter; there's pro football defensive end Zack Allen; Nick Pia of the NCPD, who taught us how to drive; Paul Setti, the caddymaster at the New Canaan Country Club; artist Mike Sasanoff; Cherry Street East; etc. (And before I go getting lots of "boos" & "hisses", Joe's Pizza.)

I hope you had as much pleasure reading this book as I did both researching & writing it.

There have been several folks I've profiled that have asked me to write more about myself & what all I've done since NCHS, so here goes:

Margot (the "t" is silent, BTW) recalled something in her Foreword that went back to when we first knew each other in the 4th grade at South School. I had broken my right arm while riding double on a bike with Brian Lueders, who lived up the street from me. A business colleague of my Dad gave me a book, "The First Book of Presidents", early on in my recovery. I was fascinated by much of it, including William Howard Taft's girth. (He allegedly got stuck in White House bathtub according to that book.) This probably began my fascination with Trivia.

Margot. If somebody mentioned her name at school, we all knew who they were talking about. Ditto Megan (pron "MEE-gan") & Pringle. I'm sure other classes had fellow students readily identifiable by their first names. But let's move on here.

I went to the American Academy of Dramatic Arts in New York City after my 1963 graduation. Performed as a professional actor in summer stock, radio commercials, & some "Off-off Broadway" showcases. This was sandwiched around a tour of duty in combat in Vietnam (1966-'67).

Returned to acting, but my heart was no longer truly in it after 'Nam. So I chucked that profession & returned to my native Buffalo, NY, in the early 1970's. Did well for myself in direct sales for a local general construction firm. Completed my education at Buffalo State College. I taught social studies at both the middle & high school levels in the suburbs of Buffalo. Was on Buffalo radio as both a news anchor & co-host of call-in talk show ("Speak Your Mind") for 2 & ½ years. Also did Development for the Buffalo Philharmonic Orchestra.

No, I never made any great fortune. I really didn't seek it. But I've certainly met many fascinating people along the way, including during my semi-retirement job at the local Sam's Club for nearly 8 years. Now I'm fulfilling a new career for myself in writing, which I've always enjoyed doing.

Yes, much of my life is worth writing about, but that's for another time. Frankly, I really enjoy living life one day at a time. I have an attitude of gratitude for what all I have.

Baseball's Casey Stengel said it best years ago: "A lot of people my age are dead at the present time". That double entendre is so true. As for me, I intend to stay active.

Ya know, gang, it's been great spending all this time with each of you.

We'll talk again.

ALAMY STOCK PHOTOS

LEE BOWMAN   Glasshouse Images

TONY GOLDWYN Storms Media Group

JENNIFER & JOEL GREY dpa picture alliance

LARRY HAGMAN AF archive

CHRISTOPHER MELONI   PictureLux/The
    Hollywood Archive

TIM ROBBINS   PictureLux/The Hollywood Archive

SUSAN SARANDON   Pictorial Press Ltd.

ALLISON WILLIAMS   dpa picture alliance

CHARLES SAXON Phillip Harrington

ANN CURRY   Everett Collection, Inc.

TERRY HANRATTY (with Nixon & O.J.)Everett
    Collection Historical

FAY VINCENT   ZUMA Press, Inc.

MIKE BRZEZINSKI & JOE SCARBOROUGH ZUMA
    Press, Inc.

PHIL DONAHUE & MARLO THOMAS   Everett
    Collection, Inc.

JIM FOWLER   WENN Rights Ltd.

RICK MOODY   Everett Collection, Inc.

GETTY IMAGES

MARY MARTIN   Hulton Deutsch/Corbis Historical

ROSEMARY RICE CBS Photo Archive

CORNELIA OTIS SKINNER   Hermann/The LIFE
   Images Collection

ARNOLD STANG   Dave Buresh/*DenverPost*

RAWLEIGH WARNER, JRThe Aschi Shimbun

"SKITCH" HENDERSON Yale Joel/The LIFE Collection

ANDRE KOSTELANETZ Bettman Collection

LILY PONS Keystone-France/Gamma-Keystone

McCOY TYNER   Jan Persson/Premium Archive

MARGARET BOURKE-WHITE The LIFE Picture Collection

FAYE EMERSON   Peter Stackpole/The LIFE
   Picture Collection

CLIFTON FADIMAN   CBS Photo Archive

JACK & MIRIAM PAAR   Hulton Archive

MADAME CHIANG KAI-SHEK Patrick Lin/AFP

ADDITIONAL PHOTO CREDITS

The 1960, '61, '62, & '63 NCHS yearbooks, *Perannos*, provided me with all photos of the EDUCATORS profiled, with the exception of Hal Baron, Jim Lewis, Rose Sasanoff, & Margaret Teeters. Their photos came from personal family collections & those of friends, with the exception of Rose Sasanoff. Her individual photo is courtesy of the *New Canaan Advertiser*.

Those same *Perannos* also provided the photos of Nancy Blair, Chet Lewis, 2 of Dave Austin, the Dixie Cats, Wilky Gilmore, the celebration of the 1962 NCHS state championship in basketball, & the 1961/'62 basketball team.

The photo of Karen Santry courtesy of Tom Eye's View Blog.

The black & white photo of Rev. Chase came from the book, "Canaan Parish 1733-2008", by William D. Gardner.

The Deli-Bake photo courtesy of the New Canaan Historical Society.

The Fairty Farm courtesy of the "If You're from New Canaan..." site on Facebook.

Stephen B. Hoyt's photo courtesy of the New Canaan Historical Society. The photo of the S.B. Hoyt Florist Shop courtesy of New Canaanite.com.

Charlie Maguire photo courtesy of the New Canaan Historical Society.

Judge Stanley P. Mead was photographed by E.J. Cyr & comes courtesy of the New Canaan Historical Society.

Margaret Cabell Self's photo courtesy of the New Canaan Historical Society.

Sister Rita's 2 photos courtesy of St. Aloysius Parish.

The Powerhouse Theatre photo courtesy of *New Canaan News*.

"Rit" Bickford's photo courtesy of NCHS 1962 class website

Syd Greenberg photo courtesy *New Canaan Patch*.

Ozzie Sweet photo courtesy of the New Canaan Historical Society.

Wilky Gilmore's encased jersey photo courtesy of NewCanaanite. com

Bo Hickey photo at Lakeview Cemetery courtesy *New Canaan Advertiser*.

Photo of Ron Northey courtesy of "The Sporting News"; photo of Tim Scott courtesy Pro Football Hall of Fame.

Herb Oscar Anderson & Jack Sterling photo provided by
   Bob VanDerHeyden.

Preston Neal Jones was photographed by Nancy O. Rich.

   The remaining photographs were generously donated by family members, friends, or by those being profiled themselves. I thank you so much for them. This was truly a team effort.

   (Oh, yes: Was unable to find pictures of either William C. Esty or Phil Jones anywhere online. Tried my best there, gang, but to no avail. Oh, well.)

ABOUT THE AUTHOR

Arthur Hahn is a 1963 graduate of New Canaan High School. He has an Associates Degree in Theatre Arts from the American Academy of Dramatic Arts. He also has a BS in Secondary Education/Social Studies from the State University College at Buffalo, NY. He has performed as a professional actor in summer stock, radio commercials, & "Off-off Broadway" showcases. He was in direct sales for a general construction firm in Buffalo. He taught social studies at both the middle & high school levels in Western New York suburbs. He was both a news anchor & co-host of a call-in talk show on Buffalo radio. He also did Development for the Buffalo Philharmonic Orchestra. Today he is a widower residing in North Charleston, SC, where he is "gainfully retired". This is his first published book.

He can be reached at nchs29418@gmail.com

Edwin Eberman